This boo w.

27 F

1

000

The
HINDUS
in
BRITAIN

Janet Swinney

B.T. Batsford Ltd, London

Contents

Illustrations
All the photographs in this book were either taken or prepared for publication by Naresh Sohal.

© Janet Swinney 1988
First published 1988

Typeset by Tek-Art Ltd, Kent
and printed in Great Britain by
R J Acford Ltd
Chichester, Sussex
for the publishers
B T Batsford Ltd
4 Fitzhardinge Street
London W1H 0AH

ISBN 0 7134 5265 X

With special thanks to Naresh Sohal, without whose knowledge and guidance this book could not have been written.

Thanks are due also to the Kapila, Rohatgi, Pandya and Ganatra families for their willingness to contribute to this book, to Des Raj Sohal and Vishnu Sharma for their help during the research and to Peter Waygood for many long hours spent at the word-processor.

Cover pictures
The colour photograph on the front cover shows a Hindu betrothal ceremony at a temple in Leicester. The background picture shows a vegetable supermarket in Wembley. The black-and-white photograph is of Amit, son of Kiritkumar and Indumati Pandya.

Introduction

This book is about the Hindus who live in Britain. It traces developments from the post-war years, when Hindus first began to come to Britain from their own countries with thoughts of making a living here, to the present day, when many young Hindus, born here, have known no other home.

The book looks at why people came to Britain, where they came from, what life was like for them before their arrival and what it has been like since. It examines some of the difficulties facing Hindus in Britain at the present time, as well as their hopes and their ambitions. It also tries to establish what makes a Hindu and what is special about the Hindu way of life. Like the term "Christian", "Hindu" can be used in two different ways – to refer to people who have a particular set of beliefs about the meaning of life, and in a more general way to refer to a certain kind of life-style associated with those beliefs. Both of these aspects of Hinduism are important.

These issues are dealt with in general terms, but the book also draws upon the experiences of four Hindu families living in different parts of the country. These four families do not represent every aspect of Hindu culture in Britain, but because of their range of backgrounds, occupations, geographical locations and personal interests, they can give us a broad understanding of Hindu life. In some ways they have a lot in common, and in other ways nothing at all.

As members of the family talk about themselves, the non-Hindu reader can get some kind of insight into what it feels like to be a Hindu in Britain today. Hindu readers, on the other hand, might find it interesting to see how their own thoughts and experiences compare with those described here.

From learning about the specific in this way it becomes possible to understand the general.

Hinduism originates from India where the majority of the population are Hindus. It is not an exclusive religion. This means that people are not kept out on racial grounds or because they have not been through a special initiation ceremony. All you have to do to be a Hindu in the religious sense is to hold several of the key beliefs that are explained in Chapter 5. Nevertheless, most of the Hindus in the world today have their roots in India. If they don't live there themselves then they generally have relatives who do.

Hinduism has its own distinctive qualities. But, having said this, it should also be pointed out that Hindus have much in common with other people who originate from the Indian sub-continent. (This means India, Pakistan, Bangladesh, Nepal and Sikkim.) For instance, Hinduism gave rise to Buddhism, Jainism and Sikhism, which are variants of it rather than contradictions, so from a religious point of view there is common ground between believers. There are also similarities which arise simply because people have lived alongside each other over a period of centuries. So, for instance, later in this book, you will see pictures of northern India where both Hindus and Sikhs are wearing turbans. The turban originated as a way of protecting the head against the sun, and any man could and still can wear it. It was only much later on that the Sikhs invested it with symbolic value as a part of their religion, and began to take special pains over what it looked like.

Even where religious thinking is substantially different from Hinduism, as with Islam and

Christianity, living alongside each other can mean that people have similar lifestyles and customs. These similarities are as apparent among the people who have come to Britain as they are in the Indian sub-continent. This point is worth remembering, because pinning labels on people and trying to make them stick can often create divisions where none existed.

In this book, the word "Asian" is used to mean people who ultimately have their roots in the Indian sub-continent regardless of their religion, present political boundaries or the route by which they came to Britain.

Why are studies like this important?

Britain is a multi-cultural society. This means that between them the people living in it have a tremendous range of skills, knowledge and experience. This wealth of resources could be used to everyone's advantage. But before we can build a positive future for ourselves in this way, each of us – whether Christian, Hindu or Muslim, black, white or brown – needs to be able to understand and appreciate what others have to offer. This means having the open-mindedness to consider what makes sense about the way other people do things and the honesty to question some of our long-standing habits and assumptions. Mutual understanding is the basis of co-operation.

There is nothing to be lost by learning about other people. On the contrary, there is a lot to be gained. This book is just to whet your appetite. The rest is up to you.

4

Who's Who – the Families

The four families who have generously contributed to this book are the Kapilas, the Rohatgis, the Pandyas and the Ganatras.

The Kapila family live in Wembley, Middlesex, in the heart of one of Britain's largest Indian communities – in this case Hindu. Parshotam (born 1941) and his wife Santosh (born 1944) come from

The Kapilas at home. From left to right – Anita, Parshotam, Santosh and Rajesh.

small towns in the Hoshiapur District of Punjab in northern India. The people living round them are mainly Hindus who have come to Britain from various parts of East Africa, but whose roots go back to the State of Gujerat in western India. Parshotam came to Britain in 1965 and was joined by Santosh in 1966. The couple have two children – Anita (born 1966) and Rajesh (born 1969). Parshotam is a postal worker at the Post Office's large Mount Pleasant sorting office; Santosh works as a sales assistant at a well-known high street store selling audio and video equipment. Anita has a job as a junior technician at a north London hospital and Rajesh is at school studying for GCE "A" levels in Physics, Chemistry and Geology.

The Rohatgi family live in Glasgow. Although there is a sizeable Asian community in the city, the Rohatgis live in a suburb where their neighbours are white. Krishna Kumar Rohatgi (born 1937) comes from the town of Patna in Bihar, north-east India, on the banks of the River Ganges. Sharad Rohatgi (born 1939), Krishna's wife, comes from the town of Poona in the State of Maharastra, western India. The Rohatgis came to Britain in 1967. Both Krishna and

Krishna Rohatgi outside his family's home in Glasgow.

Sharad are doctors. Krishna is a consultant psychiatrist at a hospital for the mentally ill in Glasgow. Sharad is in general practice in a small town in West Lothian. The couple have four sons. Raj (born 1966) is studying Civil Engineering at Glasgow University; Rahul (born 1968) is in his first year at Oxford University studying Electronic Engineering; Ravi (born 1970) is at school working for GCE "O" grades and Roshan (born 1975) is at primary school.

The Pandya family live in Edinburgh. Again, although Edinburgh has a small Asian community, the Pandyas live in an area where their neighbours are white. Kiritkumar (born 1940) and his wife Indumati (born 1944) came to Britain from Uganda in 1972. They brought with them their small daughter Alpa (born 1968). Their son, Amit, was born here in 1975. The family owns three grocery shops – the kind of corner shop that used to thrive everywhere in Britain but now only seems to flourish in Scottish towns. Kiritkumar and Indumati

Kiritkumar and Indumati Pandya in one of their shops in Edinburgh.

The Ganatra family at home: back left, Kiran; back right, Manoj; middle left, Madhukanta; middle right, Ratilal; front, Bhavna.

run one shop – the rest are managed by other people. Alpa is at Stirling University studying French and Economics. Amit is at primary school.

The Ganatra family live in Leicester, in the heart of a large and thriving Asian community – again mainly comprised of Gujerati Hindus who have come to Britain via East Africa. The Ganatras themselves come from Tanzania. Ratilal Vansanji Ganatra (born 1929) and his wife Madhukanta (born 1934) settled in Britain with their five children – four boys and a girl – in 1973. Ratilal now owns and runs a store in Leicester, selling hardware items – cooking utensils and so on – for the Asian home. Here he is greatly assisted by one of his sons, Nitin (born 1950), and sometimes by his wife. As for the rest of the family, Chandrakant (born 1951) is an anaesthetist and is on placement in Durham; Kiran (born 1960) is a dentist and works in Sheffield; Manoj (born 1964) is a pharmacist working in Leicester, and Bhavna (born 1968) is at school studying for GCE "A" levels in Economics, Mathematics and Biology.

Raj Rohatgi and Chandrakant Ganatra were away from home when this book was written, and Nitin Ganatra was occupied with family business.

Alpa Pandya on the campus of Stirling University.

2

Other Times, Other Places

Migration is not a recent phenomenon. Ever since human beings appeared on the face of the earth, they have been moving about in search of food, shelter, personal safety and a better standard of living.

The British Isles themselves have seen invasions and settlements by the Anglo-Saxons, Vikings, Romans and Norman French. They have provided refuge for people fleeing religious persecution (for example, the Protestant French "Huguenots" in the seventeenth century), and for people fleeing political persecution (in our own time, the Vietnamese "Boat People"). On the other hand, in the late eighteenth and early nineteenth centuries, many Scottish Highlanders fled from Britain to the New World countries of America and Australia, having been turned out of their homes by wealthy landowners. Where human settlement is concerned, things are always in a state of flux.

So why are there Indians in Britain? And more specifically, why are there Indians who are Hindus in Britain?

The Indian sub-continent has its own long history. There is evidence of human activity there as far back as between 400,000 and 200,000 B.C. Since then, the area has given rise to a number of major civilizations and societies. These include the Indus Valley Civilization (approximately 2300-1500 B.C.), Aryan society (approximately 1500-600 B.C.), the Mauryan Empire (321-185 B.C.), the Gupta Empire (A.D. 300-700) and the Mughal Empire (A.D. 1526-1707).

All of these periods in Indian history are worth reading about in greater detail elsewhere. They were periods of political stability during which great intellectual and social advances were made.

"This looks nice, Eric. Bring the cases".

The Indus Valley Civilization is one of the oldest known civilizations in the world. Aryan society is important because of the influence the Aryans have had upon Indian thought right up until the present day. They were, in fact, the originators of the religion and way of life now referred to as Hinduism. The Mauryan Empire is distinguished by the sophisticated systems of government and internal administration which it developed. During the Gupta Empire there were great advances in the fields of mathematics and astronomy. The astronomer Aryabhata's calculations of π, the ratio of the circumference of a circle to its diameter, and the length of the solar year were remarkably close to present day estimates, for instance. And by the fifth century A.D., Indian astronomers were regularly using the decimal system.

The Mughals were Muslim rulers. They left behind converts to Islam and some remarkable architectural achievements which include the Taj Mahal and the deserted city of Fatehpur Sikri, near Agra.

India – working in the fields.

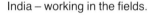

All this shows that the Indian sub-continent was in a state of progress long before the same could be said of Europe.

Throughout the history of the sub-continent, the processes of invasion and settlement continued. The Aryans themselves are thought to have been nomads from the area which is present-day Iran. The Mughals were originally from Turkey. There were many other incomers beside these, including Huns, Afghans and Mongols and even Alexander the Great, who invaded in 327 B.C. The last incomers of any major significance were the British.

From about the middle of the fifteenth century A.D., at the end of the Middle Ages, European countries vied with each other to build empires overseas. The purpose of this was to increase the wealth and power of the home country. In A.D. 1600 the British founded the British East India Company to develop their spice trade in the East Indies. The Dutch, however, defeated the company in its attempts to do this, so the British opted instead for the Indian sub-continent where they established bases in Calcutta, Madras and Bombay. At this point the Mughal Empire was in decline and there were no obvious successors. The British filled the void. They

India – spinning cotton by hand. This ancient craft, encouraged by Mahatma Gandhi, is still carried on today. The textile industry is one of India's largest.

India – a village woman milks her water buffalo. The hand-driven wheel in the background is used for chopping animal fodder.

discovered that by supporting one local ruler against another they could gradually increase their sphere of control. They continued this process until eventually most of the sub-continent was under British rule.

At first the British simply concerned themselves with conducting trade, but in 1830 a Whig government came to power in Britain. The Whigs, precursors of the Liberal Party, were interested in social and political reform, so it became policy that the East India Company should be responsible for the "welfare" of its subjects. In practice this meant building schools and colleges imparting Western knowledge through the medium of the English language, the introduction of Western medicine and English law and the intensification of Christian missionary work.

Indians began to see these innovations as a threat to their traditional way of life. In 1857, the Indian Mutiny broke out. After it was suppressed in 1858, the East India Company was disbanded and direct rule imposed from Britain under Queen Victoria.

After this, the British concentrated on developing commerce, industry, irrigation and science. Roads and railways were built. The railway system, which was almost complete by 1900, was the best in Asia.

The years 1858-1905 were the heyday of British supremacy in the Indian sub-continent. The British maintained their superiority by treating the Indians as their inferiors while the Indians, on the other hand, were overawed by the power and the technical and scientific knowledge of the British. Many Indian men were educated at English-style institutions and then went into government service in administrative jobs of one kind or another. This enabled the British to run British India with only 1200 Britons in key posts.

At this point, European intellectuals were interested in concepts such as civil liberty, equality, nationalism and constitutional government. Indians who had been educated at Western-style schools and colleges began to see that there was a large gap between what the British said they believed in and the way they behaved towards their Indian subjects. At the same time, there were growing complaints about the British feathering their own nest at the expense of the Indians.

All of this gave rise to the Indian National Congress, a movement dedicated to the idea of "India", a self-governing nation transcending the regional boundaries of the sub-continent. Congress met for the first time in 1885.

Independence eventually came in 1947. It was achieved largely as the result of an extremely effective campaign of non-violent civil disobedience led by Mohindas K. Gandhi (Mahatma Gandhi) who was prominent in the Congress movement from 1920 onwards.

One consequence of Independence was the creation of Pakistan as a homeland for Muslims. This was formed by partitioning the states of Punjab in the north-west and Bengal in the east. At Independence there was a transfer of populations, with Hindus leaving the areas allocated to Muslims and many Muslims – though not all – leaving India for the new states West Pakistan and East Pakistan (later Bangladesh). In the course of this upheaval there was a great deal of bloodshed.

Independence did not mark the end of the relationship between Britain and India. In the post-war years when Britain was short of labour to rebuild the country, immigration from the New Commonwealth countries – which included India and Pakistan – was actively encouraged. Many Indians and Pakistanis accepted the invitation. The Indians who went were mainly from the area of the Punjab, which was still Indian territory, and were either Hindus or Sikhs. The Pakistanis were, of course, Muslims.

The obvious attraction for the migrants of the post-war years was the affluent standard of living which the U.K. could offer them, compared with the relative poverty in their own parts of the world. Even a manual job in the United Kingdom could ensure a higher standard of living than a white-collar job in India. Many well educated, well qualified men were prepared to take unskilled jobs in the interest of earning a better living for themselves and their families. A further attraction was the fact that Indians had got used to the British style of doing things. They felt they would be able to work well alongside the British in the United Kingdom. It looked like a straight exchange – a better quality of life for the immigrants in exchange for a flourishing Britain with a sound industrial base.

The peak period for immigration into Britain from the Indian sub-continent was from the mid-1950s until the late 1960s. Generally the men came first, established themselves and then sent for the

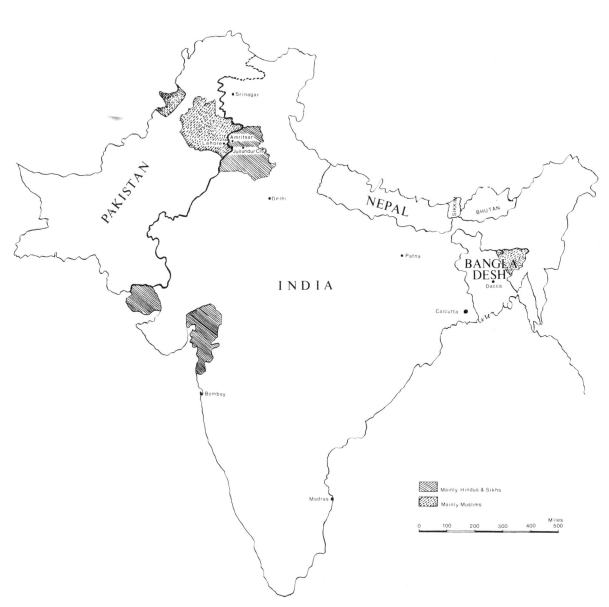

The main areas of the Indian sub-continent from which people came to Britain.

women. People settled where work was most easily available, i.e. in London and in the industrial cities of the Midlands, the north of England and Scotland. Hindus and Sikhs established themselves in West London (Southall), Manchester, Birmingham, Coventry, Leicester and Glasgow in particular.

Many people had every intention of returning to the sub-continent once they had found their feet economically, but, as we shall see, things often did not turn out that way.

The British had been busy in other parts of the globe besides India. In the last two decades of the nineteenth century, the European nations became interested in colonising the continent of Africa. Amongst other places, the British annexed land around the lake known as Lake Victoria. This area was referred to as the British East Africa Protectorates and comprised present day Kenya, Uganda and Tanzania (formerly Tanganyika and Zanzibar). Nearby Malawi and Zambia were also acquired during the nineteenth century. The process of annexing land was more or less at an end by the time the First World War started. From then until the

AFRICA

Cairo •

UGANDA
Kampala
Lake Victoria
KENYA
• Nairobi
RWANDA
BURUNDI
TANGANYIKA
Dar es Salaam ●
⊙ ZANZIBAR

Miles
0 1 2 3 4 5 6 7 8 9 1000

The areas of East Africa from which Asians came to Britain.

1960s, the European colonialists concentrated on building African nations with geographical boundaries which the colonial powers themselves had decided upon. To do this, they needed to develop their administrative and economic control.

The British dealt with this by encouraging both British settlement and settlement by people from the Indian sub-continent. From the British point of view, the Indians were a ready-made work force. Under the British in British India, they had gained know-how in the field of engineering, and in the construction of roads, railways and canals. In particular they had also undertaken administrative jobs at the lower end of the British governmental ladder and they had entered into business relationships with the British. Their skills and experience were exactly what the British needed in East Africa. It was much cheaper and quicker to import this ready-made labour force than to start all over again with the Africans.

The migrants to East Africa from the sub-continent were mainly Punjabis and Gujeratis – the latter being well known for their entrepreneurial spirit. Many of these people were Hindus.

Gradually the Africans themselves began to press for some say in the government of these newly created countries. By the second half of the twentieth century, these demands could no longer be resisted. Tanzania gained its independence in 1960, Uganda in 1962 and Kenya in 1963. It was at this point that things became difficult for many East African Asians. They were seen as supporters of the British, and beneficiaries of British rule. Having come originally from British India, many had British passports. In 1972 Uganda, under General Idi Amin,

forcibly expelled people who were from the Indian sub-continent. In other countries they were asked to commit themselves to their new nation by giving up their British passports. Overall, life became uncomfortable and it began to look as though East African Asians would lose the status they had previously enjoyed.

In these circumstances, some people returned to India. But many others who, because of their long-standing relationship with the British, now felt as much affinity with Britain as with India, went to Britain or to other Commonwealth countries instead.

These are the main routes by which there come to be Hindus in Britain. The white British themselves have never lost their fascination with the Indian sub-continent and its people. They are constantly exploring that period in their history when British India was a reality. The television series *Jewel in the Crown* and *The Far Pavilions* and films like *A Passage to India* and *Gandhi* and evidence of this.

3

New Beginnings

Parshotam and Santosh Kapila came to Britain direct from India. They went about this in a way similar to many other people who came to Britain in the 1950s and 1960s. What happened was this:

In their hometowns in Punjab, Parshotam's and Santosh's families were well respected landowners and traders. By Indian standards, they were comfortably off. Right from childhood, Parshotam had shown considerable musical talent. When he was 12, he started learning Indian classical music with a teacher. Only one year later he was able to take part in Harballabh Sangeet Mela, a major music festival held every year in Jalandhar City, in Punjab. At 15 he

Parshotam Kapila performs Indian classical music in his living room in Wembley. The instrument, a *tanpura*, is used to provide a "drone" accompaniment.

was broadcasting on All-India Radio and in his college years he came first in a number of national inter-university competitions. After college, one of India's foremost singers, Bhimsen Joshi, invited him to become his student. However, Kapila's family were not prepared to support him any longer. He had to give up any idea of furthering his musical career and concentrate instead on how to earn a living. Britain seemed like the obvious solution. "There were better opportunities to earn a bread-and-butter living in Britain than in India," he says. "That everybody knows. There's no secret." In 1965 he set off. He had one friend in the Midlands, so that's where he made for.

Before Kapila took his decision, though, the two families had arranged a marriage between him and Santosh. After they were married, Santosh stayed behind while Kapila set off for Britain. She joined him in 1966, by which time he had managed to get a job with the Post Office in London and had saved a little bit of money.

"There's no doubt about it," says Santosh, "it was a struggle living in one room in the East End of London trying to save enough money to buy a house. When I came here I couldn't speak English very well, but at least I could read a map of the London Underground and that's how I got about. Nobody, nobody should come here without the language."

Krishna and Sharad Rohatgi also came to Britain direct from India. Their reasons for coming were different from those of Kapila and Santosh. Nevertheless, there were many other people like them.

Both Krishna and Sharad came from professional

families. Krishna's father was an engineer and Sharad's a mathematician. Krishna and Sharad were both pursuing medical careers in the Indian Air Force when they met in 1963, having been stationed near each other in Delhi. They spent a large part of their social life whizzing about town on motor scooters,

Parshotam (centre back) and other members of his college with awards received for outstanding musical achievement.

The bicycle is one of the most popular forms of transport in India. This is a bicycle repair shop.

India – a busy street scene.

"which in those days," says Sharad, "was quite a novel thing to do." She adds, "That was one of the happiest times of my life."

In 1966, the couple were married. Shortly afterwards, they returned to civilian life and worked for Bihar State Medical Service on the State's family planning programme. This was hard going because of the amount of travelling involved. Things became even more difficult once Sharad had her first baby. In the meantime, Krishna had applied for and got an employment voucher for Great Britain. At that time, British qualifications were much sought after and everybody in India who was seriously interested in career advancement needed to have them. The voucher was only valid for six months, so before the time was up Krishna and Sharad had to decide what to do. In the end they decided to come to Britain even though Sharad was expecting her second baby by now and their families advised them not to leave. They arrived in 1967. With three years' leave of absence from Bihar State Medical Service they fully intended to return once they had their qualifications.

Baby number one, Raj, was left behind with Sharad's mother.

The couple had arranged for two friends to meet them at the airport when they landed. However, their plane was delayed by many hours so they arrived to find that their friends had had to go back to work. They were alone in a new country with what remained of the £3.50 the Indian Government had allowed each of them to bring with them. Their first task was to figure out how to use a British telephone – very different from an Indian one – to get someone to come and collect them. At last they succeeded!

They spent a couple of days in north London with one of their friends and then went to stay with another in Cardiff. This man gave lots of practical advice on how to go about life in Britain. He showed Krishna how to open a bank account with no money in it and explained how to arrange an overdraft facility. "And from that day to this," laughs Krishna, "I have always been overdrawn!" From here the couple moved to Coventry to take up a hospital placement which they had arranged in advance.

The Pandyas and the Ganatras are typical of the families who came to Britain from East Africa.

Kiritkumar Pandya's family emigrated from India to Uganda in 1922. His father was first a driver's

India – lessons taking place out of doors in the pleasant winter weather.

Kiritkumar Pandya (extreme left) and friends on an outing break their journey at the Equator.

mate and then a labourer on a sugar cane estate. Through hard work he managed to save enough money to buy 300 acres of land. After that he was able to think about having a family, so he got married in 1932 to a bride from India. The couple had nine children. By the time Kiritkumar grew up the family was a flourishing concern with commercial as well as agricultural interests. Kiritkumar was trained as a mechanic and managed the family's three garages.

Indumati, in the meantime, had been brought up in Kenya, as part of her sister's family. Her brother-in-law was a bank manager so she was well looked after. After she left school, Indumati got a job as a primary school teacher – which she enjoyed very much. Then the two families arranged a marriage between her and Kiritkumar, so after that she went to live with him and his family in their home town of Jinja in Uganda.

Indumati and Kiritkumar continued to live as part of this large "joint" family until their first child, Alpa, was born in 1968, when they got a home of their own. "Life was very comfortable," says Kiritkumar. "The people were very nice, it was beautiful country, there was sun, the land was very fertile and there was a good standard of living."

At this point, as part of a move to improve the state of affairs for Africans, President Milton Obote began to talk of penalising all "non-resident" businessmen by taking a greater share of their profits. Asians waited anxiously to see how they would be affected. Suddenly, in 1972, without any warning, there was a political coup and Idi Amin seized power. The army was on the streets everywhere and there was widespread looting and killing. "I have seen with my own eyes," says Kiritkumar, "the River Nile, the water red with blood, and dead bodies – black, brown, white." Immediately the order was given that Asians should leave the country in 90 days. "Ninety days in which to wind up a business. It was impossible," says Kiritkumar. "There were taxes and bills to sort out, but travel was out of the question. Even on the road between Jinja and Kampala, there were 12 road blocks on the way."

This general upheaval also coincided with personal misfortune for the family. Three weeks before the coup, Indumati had given birth to a baby boy. Twenty-five days later, the very day that the President announced that all Asians should leave the country, he died while asleep in his cot. "I hate to remember that time," says Indumati. "It was really heartache." The last couple of weeks were spent in terror. "The house was full of mourners," Indumati goes on. "At any time of day or night the army could

Members of Kiritkumar Pandya's family perform a religious ceremony in their home in Uganda after the death of his father.

just come to your door and take what they wanted. And that was what they did."

The time came to make the journey to the airport. The Pandyas were bound for Britain because they had British passports which were no longer acceptable in India. Their relatives who had Ugandan passports had to go to Canada instead. Each family was allowed to bring only 50 pounds with them. Everything else had to be left behind. Of course, many people tried to get round this restriction. Indian women invest their savings in gold jewellery. So what Indumati did was to sew some of her jewellery into an old pair of her husband's trousers and pack them in a suitcase. Off they set hoping they wouldn't be caught. Even Alpa, who was only four years old at the time, remembers the fear of being found out. Sure enough, at one of the road blocks, a soldier discovered the trousers. He started to get angry because they had insisted that they had nothing valuable with them. For a while the situation looked very unpleasant. In the end, the soldier was bought off with new clothes which the Pandyas had spent some of their savings on. So the trousers came through safely. "Everything else was

India – a lorry is loaded up with sugar cane that has just been cut, ready to go to the sugar mill.

lost," says Indumati. "We had just bought a new car in November at Diwali. It had to be left behind. I don't know what happened to it. You just leave everything in the house and walk away. It's really hard."

On arrival in Britain, the Pandya family, along with other families from Uganda were housed in a refugee camp near Bury St Edmunds. "There were about 1800 of us altogether," says Kiritkumar. "We were there 19 days in all." Indumati and Kiritkumar agree that they were very appreciative of what the white people did for them at that time. "You couldn't fault the organization," says Kiritkumar. "There were health facilities and everything in this army camp. But still it was very hard to take. When I saw the dormitory in which I would have to sleep with 40 or 50 other people, I thought I would commit suicide." "For food," Indumati goes on, "you had to queue in a huge dining hall or mess. It was all boiled potatoes and carrots. As a vegetarian, I could not even eat an egg at that time, let alone meat. And I wasn't used to having vegetables boiled in that way. I couldn't touch anything."

After a few days, the Pandyas managed to get their accommodation changed and they bumped into a friend from Uganda who told them about Sainsbury's in Bury St Edmunds. "From then on, we cooked our own food," says Kiritkumar. "We made meals out of half an aubergine, half a dozen okra and a few parathas – that kind of thing."

Eventually, Kiritkumar was called before the officer of the resettlement board. He was offered accommodation in Scotland, in Dalkeith, Midlothian. Nearly everyone else was hanging on, hoping to be offered accommodation in London. "But," he says, "I didn't even want to see the house. I looked at it this way: beggars can't be choosers."

So in 1972, in freezing weather, wearing clothes that had been given to them by the refugee agency, the family made their way north, and what Kiritkumar calls "one of life's most testing experiences" was over. "I'm not wishing to complain," says Indumati, "but what I found hardest of all was wearing those second-hand clothes that people had given us as charity."

The family arrived late at night in Dalkeith. They were met by a worker from a voluntary agency and two of the neighbours. Indumati remembers, "They had lit a big fire for us and the room was nice and

19

Dalkeith Welcomes New Citizens From Uganda

DALKEITH rolled out the red carpet on Saturday for its newest citizens — the four families of expelled Ugandan Asians who have been housed in the burgh.

A special informal reception was held for the Ugandans in the Council Chambers.

The four families are: the Dhananis (husband, wife and ten-year-old son); the Shahs (husband, wife, mother and brother); the Pandyas (husband, wife and daughter aged four and a half); and the Lachydya (mother, brother and sister).

The Dhananis and the Lachydyas were shopkeepers before their expulsion from Uganda; Mr Shah was a bookkeeper and Mr Pandyas was a service station manager.

Mr Pandyas is the only one to have obtained work so far — he took up employment at a local garage on Monday.

The families have been given houses in James Lean Avenue, Woodburn Drive, Woodburn Road and Woodburn Terrace.

Ten-year-old Naizam Dhanani has started at Woodburn Primary School and little Alpa Pandya is attending the town council's playgroup.

At Saturday's reception, Provost David Smith welcomed the families to the burgh.

GOODWILL

The Provost said the Ugandan Asians were not here in the most fortuitous of circumstances. "It is tragic that events should have compelled them to leave what had become their home and to be suddenly plunged into a strange, and, to some extent, alien world".

The Provost emphasised the difficult time which lay ahead for the Ugandans. "They are unused to our customs. They know nothing of our people. They lack many of the most basic economic necessities. They are drastically confronted with a disagreeable climate".

He stressed most people in Dalkeith were "people of goodwill" and would do all they could to "help, advise and welcome the new arrivals".

Provost Smith said he welcomed the Ugandan Asians for another reason. "All my adult life I have hated racial intolerance. A radical politician once said: "The world is my country, mankind my brethren, to do good is my religion". That's the only philosophy that is of any value in this troubled world".

He added: "Unless the world realises that there is a fundamental racial unity, there is no hope of survival".

The Provost wished the new citizens the best of luck and put his services at their disposal.

The welcome reception was attended by magistrates, councillors, and officials of the town council; and representatives of the WRVS, the Citizens' Advice Bureau, the Social Work Department, local churches, the Rotary Club, the Ladies' Circle and members of the emergency committee set up to deal with the Ugandan Asians.

Front-page coverage for the Ugandan refugees. The photograph shows Alpa Pandya and a boy from another Ugandan refugee family being welcomed to Dalkeith by the Provost. (The *Dalkeith Advertiser*, 1972)

cosy, and there was something to eat and drink. They were so very, very kind to us. But as soon as they left, it was really heartbreak. We sat looking at the bare walls, wondering what on earth we were going to do . . ."

In Tanzania, things followed a similar though not so dramatic pattern for the Ganatra family. Ratilal's family had been in East Africa since 1900. Ratilal had been sent to India to be educated. He got married there in 1948 and returned to Tanzania with his wife Madhukanta in 1950.

From this point on he worked for the family business. The family were brokers for the Government's Lint and Seed Marketing Board in Dar es Salaam. This afforded them a very comfortable living. "At one point," Ratilal remembers, "there were 20 people working for the family." All five of Ratilal and Madhukanta's children were born in Tanzania.

However, in the early 1970s, more than ten years after independence, President Julius Nyerere set about creating an African identity for the country. There was no higher education system in any case, but when the country's official language became Swahili, this made studying even harder because books were not available in the language. President Nyerere also insisted that, for life in Tanzania, any serious educational upbringing should include some time spent labouring in the fields. Ratilal and Madhukanta did not agree with this point of view. They wanted their children to have the kind of formal education that would equip them for life in the industrially advanced countries of the world. "Let's face it," says Ratilal, "with that kind of education, you can go anywhere and earn your crust."

So, reluctantly, the family agreed to leave Tanzania. Initially, in 1971, they went to India, but in 1972 Ratilal had to make a business trip to Mexico. He stopped off in Britain on the way back and liked the look of it. So, in 1973, the whole family came to Britain. Ratilal saw no reason why they shouldn't do well in the U.K. because Indians had always had privileged posts under the British in East Africa. At the same time, they had got used to white culture – so much so that Ratilal had begun to think of the way of life in India as unsophisticated. "I didn't want to go back," he says, "to be among people still wearing pyjamas!"

First of all, Ratilal bought a newsagent's business in Victoria, London, but having looked around a bit, he decided that Leicester had more to offer, so the family moved there.

The first thing that many people from the sub-continent experienced when they arrived in Britain was a sudden loss of status. The people featured in this book, for instance, all came from families that were well respected in their communities in India and East Africa. In Britain, they and many more like them became part of a brown working class that the white community had little interest in and showed no regard for. This came to many people as a great shock.

It also became clear quite quickly that the notion that the British had a higher standard of living than other people was something of a myth. It was true that, in absolute financial terms, the average Briton earned much more than someone coming from India or East Africa. But this money went to pay for goods like washing machines, electric cookers and so on – all things which you had to use yourself to carry out domestic chores. In many Indian families, including the ones described above, there had been servants to carry out these chores. So the new arrivals found that what they made up for in terms of "standard of living" they sacrificed in terms of "quality of life".

4

Making
a Go of It

From 1962 onwards, successive British governments passed laws to restrict immigration. The most stringent of these was the 1971 Immigration Act which reduced the number of men accepted for settlement and made it more difficult for those who had settled to bring their families into the country.

Those who were here, however, were busy trying to make a go of it. Many Asians, whether Hindu or Muslim, had rapidly discovered that Britain was not the land of milk and honey they had been led to expect. There was racial discrimination over jobs, homes and in the street generally. Krishna Rohatgi describes what happened when the placement at the Coventry hospital was coming to an end and he and Sharad began to look around for permanent jobs:

"We applied for about a hundred jobs each, but we weren't getting anywhere fast, so we went to see the Postgraduate Dean who was supposed to help with these matters. He was very rude. He gave us all sorts of excuses – 'I can't promise anything, things are very difficult, you've come at the wrong time etc., etc.' I pointed out that we really needed his help but that his approach was very off-putting. I asked him, could he not be more helpful? That must have rattled him, coming from a junior doctor to a very senior one. 'Look,' he said in a very derogatory and offensive manner, 'why don't you just sell your wife's jewellery?'

An Indian supermarket in Wembley.

An Indian sweet shop in Leicester.

"I was stunned that somebody should suggest we should part with our only assets. I telephoned home several times for reassurance. Several members of my family were U.K.-returned and had great faith in this country. I have them to thank for keeping me going."

The result of this kind of experience was that people from the sub-continent tended to stick together – Hindus with Hindus and Muslims with Muslims – and to rely on each other for help. This was where the Asian sense of community came into its own.

Many Hindus had lived as part of a joint family before coming to Britain. A joint family is one where the father, mother, all their sons and daughters-in-law, any unmarried daughters and all the children of the sons and daughters-in-law live together in the same household. There may even be older relatives on the man's side of the family present. The family is run as a sort of collective. Everyone has their work to do – the men earning money which is put to the use of the whole family, the women running the house. As Sharad Rohatgi explains, "There are no written

rules, but everyone knows what to do." There are many advantages to the system. For instance, children are never short of playmates, parents are never short of baby-sitters and elderly members of the family can afford to take things easy. One of the most important advantages is that support and advice are always available for those who need it. Even where one of the sons of the family moves out to a new home with his wife, the link with the parental home remains a strong one.

Beyond the joint family itself, there are links with more distant relatives, all of which are carefully maintained. There is also a bond between people from the same village whose families have lived and worked alongside each other for generations. Over and above this, of course, there are personal friends. People brought up in this kind of community have a lifelong sense of responsibility for each other. Each individual is part of an extensive network of support.

When Hindu men came to Britain, they looked around for any members of their support network who might already be here – close relatives first and then others. In the absence of these, simply being Hindu was enough to unite people in the face of racial discrimination. Even people who would not normally have mixed in India or East Africa because

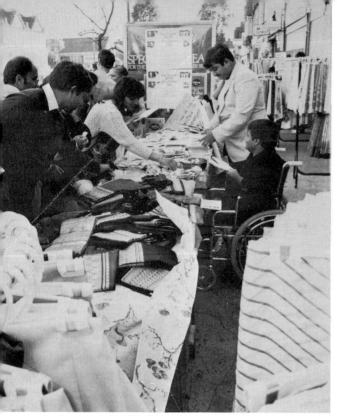

Saris on sale in Wembley.

they belonged to different castes (see Chapter 6), found themselves in a position where they welcomed each other's assistance.

It was very difficult, for instance, for Asians to get council houses. This meant that to get long-term accommodation they had to buy it. But no one had enough money for the deposit on a house. So what happened, typically, in the early days was this: someone, a Hindu, who had managed to save more than his friends or relatives, would borrow the money from them to cover the cost of the deposit. Once he had the property, he would let out as much space as possible to fellow Hindus – perhaps some of the same friends and relatives. These men would spend most of their time at work trying to earn as much money as possible and the house would be used simply as a dormitory and cookhouse. Very little was spent on leisure activities because the men worked such long hours they were too exhausted to think of doing anything else when they got home. In this way, money was saved relatively quickly. Soon, the next person was ready to move out and the process could start over again.

Money was repaid when the borrower could afford to return it or when the lender couldn't

manage without it any longer. No written records were kept. Generally, the level of trust and reliability was very high. This system proved to be a life-line for many newcomers to this country. Once the men had this kind of foothold, they could think of sending for their wives and children and other dependents to join them.

Racial discrimination in the workplace led many Asians to think about becoming self-employed. Again, the capital was often raised by borrowing money from friends and relatives who were paid back later once the business became profitable.

The same sense of collective responsibility enabled the Indian Workers' Association to raise enough money from Indians living in Southall to buy the Dominion Cinema. This became the first cinema in Britain used exclusively for the showing of Indian films.

Of course, not everyone followed the same path. When it came to buying a house, Parshotam and Santosh lost money in a deal that went wrong – a matter they don't like to talk about even today. Parshotam did not consider self-employment. The job at the Post Office brought in a steady income, so he kept at it. Santosh, in the meantime, did her best to supplement their earnings in whatever way she could. While she was expecting her first child, she attended classes at a tailoring school in Shoreditch where she learned how to use industrial sewing machines, buttonholers, overlockers and so on. After this she got her first job – in a clothing factory where she earned £5 per week as a thread cutter. She stopped for a while when her baby, Anita, was born. Then a white neighbour offered to babysit so that she could go back to work again. Not long after this, Rajesh was born. After that, Santosh stayed at home until the two children were old enough to cross the road themselves.

The support system which had worked so well for men was not so effective when it came to women. While Parshotam was out at work all day and Santosh was at home, she found herself in the same position as many other women from the Indian sub-continent who were sent for by their husbands in the 1950s and 1960s. That is, she was completely isolated. She describes the time when she was at home by herself in their one room and pregnant for the first time as, "frightening, very frightening."

Krishna Rohatgi eventually got a job in a hospital

in Cumbria as a trainee psychiatrist, so he and Sharad moved north. Many other Asian doctors also ended up in either psychiatry or geriatrics at this point, because these were the least popular areas of medicine as far as the white British were concerned.

Following this, both Krishna and Sharad got jobs in Dumfries where they stayed for the next eight years. Sharad pursued her medical career in between having babies. Like Santosh and Parshotam, Sharad and Krishna were fairly isolated. Sharad had no relatives close-to-hand who could help her with looking after the children, so she had to make other arrangements. Sharad's mother visited Britain in 1968. When Rahul was born, she took him back with her to India where she was already bringing up Raj. Later on, when Ravi was born in 1972, he was fostered out to an English friend of Sharad's in Manchester. That same year Sharad gained her membership of the Royal College of Obstetricians. The three children re-joined their parents in 1975, when Sharad's mother felt she was getting too old to look after the older two, and the friend in Manchester decided she would like to go back to work again. Another thing that happened in 1975 was that Rohan was born.

Sharad agrees that her handling of this might look fairly unusual from a typical British point of view, but she explains it this way:

"In India it is not uncommon for a family to let a daughter study and to look after her children for her, if it is in the interests of the family in the long-run. Indian parents do tend to do a lot of sacrificing for

The Ganatra hardware store.

their children. So it is not uncommon for an Indian girl to send her children back home to her mother until they are about five years old, because if you are working, naturally, you can't give that much attention to children. Nowadays, most families are a single unit, so the same thing doesn't work. But in those days, well, not everyone did it, but it wasn't looked upon as something odd. This is one of the advantages of the joint family."

By the time the Pandyas and the Ganatras arrived in Britain, Asian men had a reputation for being astute, reliable and enterprising in business. Ratial Ganatra assesses the situation:

"It wasn't difficult for people from East Africa to get bank loans. As far as the bank was concerned they were not a risk. They had the joint family supporting them, they were honest, they would do anything to avoid bankruptcy and in any financial crisis they would always make sure they paid the bank off first. What's more, they led a very inexpensive social life compared with the British. From the bank's view, there could be no better guarantees."

He himself also found that his family's reputation in Tanzania stood him in good stead when he came to Britain, and that he had no difficulty in establishing himself in the business community in Leicester. From then on, it was a case of tending the business carefully and expanding it when the chance arose.

The Pandyas got off to a rather different start. The day after the family arrived in Dalkeith, Kiritkumar went out in the bitter cold winter weather to try the local garages for a job. "I looked," he says, "just like the guy who works in the circus, with a big checked cloth hat and the clothes they had given us at the camp."

At the second garage, having looked at all Kiritkumar's Esso certificates, the owner was sympathetic. He asked Kiritkumar what kind of job he was looking for. Kiritkumar pointed out that up till now he had always been his own boss – but he was willing and able to do any job, from floor-sweeper to manager. "The choice is yours, the pleasure is mine," he added. The owner must have been disarmed by this – he took him on as a storesman.

Not long after this, the Pandya family had an experience which demonstrated that though racism was common in Britain, it was not the rule. Indumati describes it:

"It was our first Christmas in Dalkeith. You won't believe it. The *whole street* came with a gift for Alpa. I was the only one in the street who had a child, you see – the rest were old people. Everyone brought something, even if it was just a sweetie. Then there was Santa Claus. They came about half-past eight at night and knocked on the door. They said, 'Bring your little girl,' and made her sit on his lap and everything. It was just great – really great – it strikes me even now – to know that everybody was thinking about your child at that time."

Kiritkumar stayed in his job at the garage for a number of years. Meanwhile, Indumati supplemented the family income by getting a part-time job in a shop. Then she did a secretarial course and got a clerical job in the Department of Food and Fisheries.

However, financially, things were very tight. In 1975, Amit was born. "By Jove, we had a rough ride then," says Kiritkumar. "It was just hand to mouth. If you got chapatti – no dal; if you got dal – no bloody chapatti."

It was at this point that Kiritkumar decided be must do something about trying to set up business on his own. From then on, the theory put forward by Ratilal Ganatra seems to have held good.

Despite the fact that the Pandyas savings totalled a mere £132.90, a new manager at the local bank was prepared to offer Kiritkumar a £10,000 loan, unsecured, for a trial period of six months. This enabled Kiritkumar to buy a shop in Edinburgh which he ran as an off-licence cum newsagent's cum grocery store. For the next 18 months, he worked in the shop from six o'clock in the morning until nine o'clock at night, seven days a week. Indumati helped out as much as she could. The baby slept in the back of the shop while they worked.

When the first six months were up, the bank was favourably impressed. After that they were always willing to offer financial support so that Kiritkumar could extend his business interests. In this way, he was able to begin a process of leasing out a shop as soon as it was profitable and buying up another one. The family were also able to buy their own house in Edinburgh.

For the first generation of Hindu settlers, the years of struggle are more or less over. The vast majority of families now have an established source of income and have evolved for themselves a lifestyle that has a certain familiarity and regularity about it.

The Kapilas got their house soon after Rajesh was born, and have worked since to keep it well maintained.

The Rohatgi's plans to return to India faded because by the time Krishna got his membership of the Royal College of Physicians, the children were already settled in Britain. "It was not our fate," says Sharad. Lots of other people found themselves in the same sort of situation.

Krishna is now a consultant psychiatrist at a hospital in Glasgow. On reflection, he feels that the move into psychiatry was not a bad thing: "This is a speciality where we Asians tend to do slightly better. Hindus have a sort of blind faith in God which in times of stress gives rest to the mind."

Sharad went on to study for a Diploma in Community Medicine and from there moved into general practice in West Lothian.

The Pandyas are now on the look-out for a restaurant which they could develop. Their hours of work, running one shop and keeping an eye on two others, are still very long, with very little time for leisure. Kiritkumar reckons that it will be another five years before they can afford to take things a bit more easily.

Ratilal Ganatra has reached the position where he can spend almost as much time on other matters as on his own business. He is involved in numerous organisations concerned with promoting the welfare of Hindus in Britain. These include the Mahatma Gandhi Foundation and the Foundation of Indian Associations, of which he is President. He was formerly the vice-chairman of the Community Relations Council in Leicester, and is a regular attender at events in the Hindu community.

Most first-generation Hindu settlers now also have children who are either grown up and have taken their place in the work-force, or are well on the way to doing so. The situation in our four families is fairly typical. The four Ganatra sons are already well-established in their careers, and Anita Kapila has started on hers too. For the rest of the younger generation, studying and getting qualifications is the name of the game. All of them are pretty clear about their career ambitions. Bhavna Ganatra's aim is to become an accountant. Alpa Pandya wants a career

In her spare time, Anita Kapila is studying for an HND.

where her knowledge of languages will be used – either in professional interpreting or in business. Rajesh Kapila is considering either geochemistry or sound recording. In the Rohatgi family, Raj and Rahul are well on the way to becoming civil and electronics engineers respectively, while Ravi thinks he may opt for petrochemical engineering.

Even the younger children have plans. Amit Pandya has his heart set on being a sports physiotherapist, while Roshan Rohatgi's burning ambition is to be an American footballer.

The children, it would seem, are building on the hard work of their parents, and are well on the way to turning their parents' hopes for them into reality.

5

Hinduism
as a Religion

The Philosophy

The term "Hindu" was invented by the Muslims who invaded the Indian sub-continent from Turkey and Afghanistan. They used the word simply as a means of distinguishing between themselves and the non-Muslim people they ruled over – the people of "Hindstan", or India.

In fact, what we now refer to as Hinduism is a complex philosophical tradition which has been evolving since the Vedic, or Aryan, period (see Chapter 2) and which is expressed through a wide range of practices.

The Aryans produced the first literary works in Indian history. These were the "Vedas". These writings include hymns, prayers and information about social responsibilities, rituals, magical formulae, medicine and astronomy. In the later part of the period, a series of commentaries on the "Vedas", called the "Upanishads", was begun. The works, taken as a whole, show how, starting from the idea that elements such as fire, sun and wind were gods, the Aryans gradually evolved a concept of God as a universal force, pervading everything.

If the universal force pervades everything, then it follows that this must include human beings, and that they like everything else in this world, both animate and inanimate, are material expressions of

Varanasi (Benares) on the bank of the River Ganges. The Ganges is considered important for symbolic reasons. Many people come here to pray, and many bodies are cremated here.

an abstract force. This means that God exists both inside and out of each individual.

This view that the energy within each person is the same as the energy which drives the Universe is the first and most important belief of Hinduism. It was first formulated in "Vedanta", a system of thought which evolved towards the end of the Aryan period (and which means, literally, "the final part of the Vedas"). Although various schools of philosophy have developed since that time, this is the starting point for all of them. This fundamental belief is expressed in the statement *Tat tvam asi*, which means, literally, "That art Thou", or "Truth is within us."

The universal force as it occurs in the abstract, is known as *Brahman*. As it occurs in the individual person, it is known as *Atman*. *Atman*'s natural tendency is to re-unite with *Brahman*. When this happens, the person concerned experiences a state of transcendental bliss. But, it doesn't happen easily because the *Atman* is trapped in a physical form which is constantly engaged in activity involving pain and pleasure which human beings often regard as ends in themselves. In the circumstances, the only way that union can be achieved is as a result of a process of self-awakening, or spiritual development. The attainment of union is the whole purpose of human existence.

The Sanskrit name for the state of union, or enlightenment as it is known in English, is *moksha*. (Sanskrit is the language of the "Vedas" and "Upanishads".) *Moksha* is something that has to be experienced. You have to make it a reality in your own life. It is not a state of intellectual understanding, and no one else can experience it on your behalf. Each person is responsible for achieving *moksha* through his or her own efforts.

The attainment of *moksha* is the culmination, or end, of a process of spiritual evolution spanning numerous lifetimes. If someone fails to attain *moksha* in this life, the *Atman* will be translated into another physical form so that the development of consciousness can continue. This cycle of death and rebirth is known as reincarnation.

Whatever you do (or are) in the course of existing in this physical dimension is called *karma*. *Karma* has consequences – good and bad – for your spiritual development. The form that the *Atman* takes on at rebirth will depend on the level of spiritual development you have achieved over previous lives as the result of *karma*. In the general scheme of things, human beings are ranked higher than other creatures. This is because human beings have the greatest capacity for developing their own consciousness and for realising their divine nature. So, where there has been spiritual development, the *Atman* is likely to be reincarnated in a human form in which further development and ultimately *moksha* is a possibility. If, on the other hand, there has been spiritual regression, the opposite of development, the *Atman* may be reincarnated in a lower form.

Each newborn creature inherits the level of self-awareness developed over the *Atman*'s previous incarnations. This explains why there are some people who become enlightened at a very early age, like J. Krishnamurti, for instance. Born in 1896, he died in 1985, and is well known in the West for his teachings, recorded in books such as the *Penguin Krishnamurti Reader*, published in 1970.

The Paths

There are four *yogas*, or paths, which can be followed in order to attain *moksha*. These are not compulsory: they are simply available. The four paths are as follows:

The shore temple at Mahabalipuram, South India.

Jnana Yoga

This is the path of knowledge where what is learned through intellectual insight is translated into experience. Knowing is being. If you truly know something, you are it.

Bhakti Yoga

This is the path of devotion. The devotee achieves enlightenment through love for a personal god. The personal god is believed to be the reincarnation of *Brahman*, the universal force, and is, therefore an enlightened being. He or she represents a particular aspect of *Brahman*. Most adherents of *bhakti* are either Vaishnavites (followers of Vishnu, the Preserver), or Shaivites (followers of Shiva, the Destroyer and Recreator). Vaishnavites are divided into those who worship Lord Rama and those who worship Lord Krishna, both of whom are believed to be reincarnations of Vishnu. Through total surrender to the personal god, the devotee achieves union with that god, and ultimately with *Brahman*. Guru Nanak (A.D. 1469-1538) the founder of the Sikh movement, was a *bhakti* yogi (follower – see opposite). Hindus consider Christianity to be a form of *bhakti* yoga, because salvation is achieved through devotion to Christ.

Karma Yoga

This is the path of duty or right action. Someone who pursues this path sets out to fulfil all the social and domestic responsibilities (called *dharma*) attached to his or her particular role in life. Only if this action is carried out mindfully and with dedication can it be effective. Mahatma Gandhi (see Chapter 2) was a *karma* yogi.

Raja Yoga

This is the path of meditation. Through careful practice, it is possible to control the mind so that it looks steadily inwards. As everyday mental activity ceases, and the mind becomes stiller and calmer, the *Atman* reveals itself and *Atman*-consciousness develops. Eventually, *Atman* and *Brahman* are united. This is a description of what it is like to meditate effectively:

". . . because the pendulum moves, the clock remains alive. . . . If the pendulum stays in the middle, the clock stops. So is the mind: if you move from one extreme to another extreme, the mind continues, time continues. Mind and time are synonymous. The moment you stop in the middle time disappears, the clock stops; mind disappears, the mind stops. And in that moment, when there is no mind and no time, suddenly you become aware for the first time of who you are. All clouds have disappeared and the sky is open and the sun is shining bright." (Bhagwan Shree Rajneesh in *The Secret of Secrets*, published by the Rajneesh Foundation International 1983.)

For most people, getting the pendulum to stop is a lengthy process which must be tackled systematically and regularly, in the same way that you would practice a musical instrument, or train for sport.

Hatha yoga and *pranayama* are two components of *raja yoga* which facilitate the practice of meditation.

Hatha yoga is a physical discipline for which no equipment is necessary. It involves poses and exercises which make use of the body's own capacity for being in situations where one part counterbalances another, or where one part can be locked in tension with another. Doing this kind of yoga is like bull-working without the bullworker and massage without the masseur. The emphasis is on holding poses rather than on moving quickly in and out of them – unlike most western-style keep-fit routines. This slowness in pace has meant that *hatha yoga* has become very popular in the United Kingdom as a way of keeping fit. Although it certainly has this effect, its main purpose is to develop the physical strength and awareness, the mental calm and quietness of breathing that make it possible to sit in a meditative posture for long periods of time.

Pranayama is a discipline concerned with the control of breath. Although it can be used to enhance certain aspects of mental functioning (for example memory), its main aim is to bring about mental tranquility and to enable those who practise it to sit for long periods of time without being disturbed or distracted by the breathing process.

Raja yoga and its associated disciplines evolved over thousands of years. The first systematic account of what it involves was given in the "Yoga Sutras" by Patanjali, which date from 200 B.C.

The four paths described are not mutually exclusive. One person may pursue several of them and,

Hatha yoga being taught at the Iyengar Yoga Centre, Edinburgh.

throughout the history of the Indian sub-continent, followers of the various paths have co-existed. Someone who sets out to follow one or other of these paths is called a *yogi*. Someone who teaches others how to follow a path is called a *guru*.

Literature

There are a number of written works which have been an inspiration to Hindus over the centuries. These include the epic works, the *Ramayana* and the *Mahabharata* which appeared in their finished versions in the period 200 B.C. – A.D. 300. These works have the same sort of status for Hindus as the gospels do for Christians. The *Mahabharata* is the longest single poem in the world. Both works are accounts of episodes concerning Hindu royalty which probably took place between 1000 B.C. and 700 B.C.

The *Ramayana* is about Lord Rama and his wife Sita and, in particular, Lord Rama's struggle to rescue Sita from Ravana, the King of Ceylon (now Sri Lanka). Lord Rama's own kingdom was the kingdom of Ayodhya in the Ganges plain.

The *Mahabharata* tells of the fight between the Kaurava and Pandava families for the throne of Indraprasta (modern Delhi). It includes the *Bhagavad Gita* (Song of God) in which Lord Krishna, from Gujerat, explains to Arjun, a prince of the Pandava family, the meaning of life and how salvation can be achieved.

How far the *Ramayana* and the *Mahabharata* are based on fact is a matter that historians debate. The importance of the works is that through the characters and events they portray, they make it easy for people to understand the philosophies and principles set out in the "Vedas". The characters display personal qualities and behaviour that ordinary people can use as examples, while the *Bhagavad Gita*, for instance, explains the importance of all the different paths described above and provides instructions on how to meditate.

◁ Lord Shiva as he is popularly represented.

Rama and Sita.

Hinduism Day to Day

The fundamental belief that the Truth is within all of us explains much about Hindu behaviour and attitudes. It explains, for example, the attitude towards other religions, which is that they must be tolerated. All religions are considered to be attempts to deepen humankind's relationship with the one, same, all-pervasive God, and, therefore, to have some intrinsic merit. Although other religions are viewed as different from Hinduism, they are not thought to be incompatible with it. It is only logical, therefore, that people of other faiths should be tolerated and their beliefs respected. Tolerance is a value which, traditionally, has been highly regarded in Hindu society.

◁ Lord Krishna.

Betrothal ceremony.

The same belief accounts for the respect Hindus have for life in all its forms and for the doctrine of *ahimsa* (non-violence) which is meant to apply in dealings with all living creatures.

As religion is considered to be a matter for the individual, there is little congregational worship in Hindu temples. People who are followers of a personal god are likely to begin the day with *puja* (prayer). They may also visit a temple occasionally to make an offering and to pray. There are many ceremonies associated with important points in the human life cycle – birth, coming of age, betrothal, marriage, death, etc. In India these rites of passage are generally carried out in the home, with the assistance of a priest (*brahmin*). In Britain, where houses are more cramped for space and you can't rely on the weather to be able to hold events out-of-doors, people tend either to use the temple or some other kind of public hall.

Other than this, there are a number of religious festivals which take place during the course of the year. The most widely celebrated are: Dussehra, Durga Puja, Diwali and Holi.

Dussehra and Durga Puja both take place in October. Dussehra commemorates the time when

Durga puja celebrations; a small shrine stands in the centre of the room.

Lord Rama fought with King Ravana and was victorious. Celebrations take place over ten days, during which the story of the *Ramayana* is enacted in dramatic form. On the tenth day, an image of King Ravana is burned.

Durga Puja involves four days of worship, after which images of the warrior goddess Durga are immersed in lakes and rivers.

(Diwali takes place in November) and commemorates Lord Rama's return from banishment to his kingdom of Ayodhya. Welcoming lights are displayed around houses and public buildings, and fireworks are let off.

(Holi is a festival of colour which takes place in March.) People throw coloured water and powder over each other. Basically, it is an opportunity for a good deal of rough and tumble.

In practise, as with any other religion, it is only a minority of Hindus who devote themselves wholeheartedly to following one or more of the *yogas*. For the majority, religion is a question of trying to fulfil one's *dharma* by leading a good life and conforming to social custom, in the hope that this will secure well-being in this life and a good condition in the next. Many people also have a personal god whom they pray to daily. Apart from this, there is a great deal of respect for those people who are thought to be enlightened or well on the way to achieving enlightenment. Yogis, gurus and priests are welcome visitors in most homes. When there is a guest of this sort, friends and neighbours gather to ask for blessings, to seek advice and to join in prayers.

This describes the position of Hindus in India and of many Hindus in Britain too. With some variations, it also applies to the families who feature in this book. Most members of our four families regard themselves as Hindu in the religious sense of the word. The exceptions are the children in the Rohatgi household who, having been brought up in a non-Hindu environment and attended schools where Christianity was the norm, consider themselves as "probably more Christian than anything else".

No one in these families would claim to be versed in Hindu scripture. Nevertheless, there are certain beliefs which are commonly and firmly held. Everyone, for instance, believes in God and believes that there is only one God. Indumati Pandya puts it this way: "God is one in all forms whether this be Krishna or Jesus Christ or whatever. The way you see is a different way of seeing, but God is just one. You can see God in any place you want." Others echo this view. Even Rahul and Ravi Rohatgi, who know very little about what Hinduism entails, are clear on this point.

The fact that this belief is so firmly held means that there is an automatic acceptance of other people's

Diwali – the start of another year. Members of the business community bring their accounts books to the temple to ask for blessings on future transactions.

religions. Both Parshotam Kapila and Kiritkumar Pandya, who would never contemplate giving up Hinduism, acknowledge that religion is an accident of birth – they could easily have been something else. Ratilal Ganatra says, "All religions deserve respect – the principles are the same," and Kiran adds, "It's a crime to break someone else's religion." The feeling that the form religion takes is irrelevant and that what really matters is having faith led Sharad Rohatgi to decide to give her sons a free hand. "I've given them full independence as to religion," she says. "I'm not going to force anything on them."

Everyone is also clear about the importance of *dharma*, although they don't necessarily call it that. Alpa Pandya says, "The way to God is really by helping the people who are around you." And Kiran Ganatra feels that Hinduism, without being dogmatic, offers a code you can live by. Kiritkumar Pandya aims to live his life so that even if he dies tomorrow people will remember him as "helpful, nice and good thinking". Parshotam Kapila has become a follower of Sai Baba, who is believed by many people to be an incarnation of God. He feels that his faith in Sai Baba has helped him renew his commitment to be "helpful towards others in practical ways". For Ratilal Ganatra, being involved in public life obviously provides many opportunities to fulfil *dharma*.

As far as reincarnation is concerned, the views are mixed. Most members of the four families believe in it, but Kiritkumar and Indumati Pandya feel they don't know enough to be able to make their minds up, while Rahul and Ravi Rohatgi, under Christian influence, dismiss it altogether.

The notion of *karma*, however, is widely accepted. Krishna Rohatgi says: "It really is constantly hanging over your head to keep you under control. If your *karma* is bad, you are accordingly rewarded or punished. It goes a long way in maintaining your self-discipline, and in prompting you to do what is socially acceptable, like speaking the truth, helping others, being kind and so on." Even in the case of Kiritkumar and Indumati Pandya, who are uncertain about the possibility of future lives, there is a belief that even in the course of this lifetime – "As ye sow, so shall ye reap."

When it comes to religious practice, nearly all the older generation start the day with a bath followed by *Puja*. This is usually done in front of a small shrine in some corner of the house. Sometimes *agarbatti* (incense sticks) are lit to purify the air and sometimes pictures or images of a particular personal god are used to help focus the concentration. The Ganatra family, for example, believe themselves to be direct descendants of Lord Rama, therefore Ratilal and Madhukanta pray before an image of Lord Rama. Ratilal recites a popular *mantra* from the "Vedas" called the "Gayatri Mantra". Sharad Rohatgi's family are traditionally worshippers of Lord Shiva, so she prays before an image of Lord Ganesh, the elephant god, son of Lord Shiva. She also recites a couplet from a Sanskrit work called *Rama Raksha*. Kiritkumar Pandya, on the other hand, does his *puja* in the evening. He uses nothing at all, but simply asks, "If I have done anything wrong within the last 24 hours, please forgive me. Give me peace, prosperity and the strength to survive in this funny old world."

Practice among the younger generation is much more erratic, with only one or two like Amit Pandya praying regularly at the family shrine. Ravi Rohatgi prays occasionally when he feels he has "fouled up" on something. His prayers are addressed to God via Christ. Anita and Rajesh Kapila do not pray regularly either, but they do take an interest in the videos which their father brings home which show Sai Baba performing miracles.

The families vary considerably in their public involvement in religious life. In Leicester, there is some kind of religious celebration every month and the Ganatra family attend regularly. The feeling of belonging to a community and being able to participate in these events is something which Bhavna, in particular, really appreciates. The other families seldom go to a temple and even major festivals like Diwali – if they are celebrated at all – are celebrated in the home. Amit Pandya, however, looks forward to the day when he can know more about his religion and attend the temple regularly. Despite these differences in lifestyle, there is general agreement on one point – going to the temple means nothing if your heart's not in it.

There is some musing by parents about how well they are teaching their offspring about Hinduism. It seems that the younger generation are absorbing some aspects of Hindu belief almost by accident and without much understanding of the overall philosophy. "Yes," says Krishna Rohatgi, "it's a

Diwali lights in Leicester.

Swami Mohandas, a *yogi* from Jalandhar District of Punjab, leads a prayer meeting in a house in Manchester.

subject I think about a lot, but about which I do very little." Ratilal Ganatra's approach is to involve his family directly in religious celebrations. This, he thinks, is better than any amount of lecturing.

Should a knowledge of Hinduism be taught in school? "No," say the younger generation flatly. "This is a beef our parents have rather than us. Religion is a matter for the home."

Hindu temple in Leicester.

6

Hinduism as a Way of Life – Kith and Kin

The Family

The family is the centre of activity in Hindu society. This is true even though the joint family is by no means as common as it used to be. In India, among the middle classes, there is a tendency for sons and their wives to move out of the parental home as soon as they can afford to, or to go elsewhere in search of work. The trend towards a smaller family unit is even more apparent in Britain. In the first place, the move to Britain from the Indian sub-continent fragmented most Hindu families. Secondly, although there are now two and even three generations of Hindus living in Britain, British houses are usually too small to allow all the members of one family to live together under the same roof.

Nevertheless, many of the traditions of the joint family persist. Although these days family members tend not to pool their money on a day-to-day basis, there is still financial support available for anyone who needs it in special circumstances. The family is still the place where, as Krishna Rohatgi puts it, "advice is given and usually taken", where elders are respected as well as looked after, and where keeping children amused is the responsibility of whichever adult happens to be on hand. We have already seen (in Chapter 5) that religious activity, both public and private, takes place in the home. In addition, the family is the springboard for many business ventures and the focus for a great deal of social activity.

It is not surprising, then, that "family" is an important concept for most Hindus. They derive their sense of identity from being part of this collective body. "There is no such thing," says Kiran Ganatra, "as pleasing yourself as an individual." The family must come first. Generally speaking, the notion of "family" inspires a sense of honour, a readiness to listen to other people's points of view and a feeling that there is a reputation to be maintained.

Of the four families who appear in this book, none is a joint family. The Ganatras, however, have an extensive family network which they use to full effect. Ratilal has a brother in London and one in the United States. There are regular and frequent phone calls and letters between the various parts of the family to exchange news, discuss business propositions and sort out family problems. The Leicester and London branches of the family also visit each other regularly – about once a month. If there are any special events in the offing – a marriage for example – then a full-scale family gathering will be organised. "This is notwithstanding the fact," says Kiran, "that the pace of life is much busier than in Tanzania and that these things are much more difficult to arrange."

The Ganatra offspring are beginning to move away from their base, but close contact is still maintained. Kiran, for example, works in Sheffield during the week but returns, every weekend, to Leicester where his father has bought him a house.

The Pandyas have a similar sort of network, but do not operate it with anything like the same sort of intensity. Kiritkumar has brothers in Kent and in Canada. His mother lives with his brother in Kent, but pays regular and lengthy visits to the other branches of the family. Her skills in diplomacy are fully appreciated. Kiritkumar refers to her as the family's "roving ambassador". Despite this level of support, Indumati wishes that, on a day-to-day basis, contact with other members of the family could be closer.

The Rohatgis are much more isolated than this. Sharad occasionally confers with her father in India on matters concerning Raj and Rahul, bearing in mind, she says, that they had a "dual upbringing and my father is an interested party". Other than that, she and Krishna are self-reliant. However, even this amount of consultation becomes more difficult as time goes on. "My father doesn't understand about the British way of life," says Sharad. "I come home from work at six o'clock and these boys haven't washed a cup. How can I expect him to understand that that's a problem when he's never had to make a cup of tea in his life?"

Like Indumati, Sharad laments the fact that she can't have closer contact with her relatives. She says, "I don't have any physical support if something goes wrong. If I'm not well, I'm not well . . ." Being isolated means that there are other kinds of pressure too:

"Being a foreigner in a foreign country, I think you feel even more responsible. In India, suppose one of them [the boys] gave up university, it wouldn't worry me the way it would if it happened here. Here, I wouldn't know what to do with him, I would really panic. But in India there would be friends and relatives to pressure him, to advise him."

In sharp contrast, the Kapilas have a definite preference for sorting out their own troubles and are wary of anything that smacks of interference. Parshotam occasionally visits his relatives in India – last time he took Rajesh with him – but other than that contact is minimal. Santosh believes that an extended family can be the cause of intrigue and meaningless arguments, rather than support.

The expectation that "the family must come first" is a potential source of conflict for young Hindus in Britain where both education and popular culture emphasise personal fulfilment, the rights of the individual, and so on. No doubt many young Hindus are aware of these two differing kinds of pressure. But self-fulfilment and family obligations are not necessarily incompatible and, when it comes to making plans for the future, most parents and children manage to agree on a course of action which is acceptable to both sides. Parents make allowances for the fact that their children are growing up in a society which is different from the one they grew up in and children bear in mind that "parents know

best." So, for example, Anita Kapila's parents push her to work hard at her studies and not to bother with boys until later and she is prepared to accept this because she feels that her parents have her own best interests at heart. "They are good parents," she says, "I wouldn't be who I am if it wasn't for them."

Ravi Rohatgi compares his own parents with the parents of his white British friends and comes to the conclusion that Indian parenthood has something to commend it. He sees that white parents are much less formal with their children than his own parents are. But when it comes to seeking help with problems he thinks this "matey-ness" is something of a deterrent. "If I had British parents and I told them some small problem that had been bothering me for the whole of my life, I would be afraid that they might just laugh in my face."

He thinks this informality might have the same effect on his white friends. "I find that my friends solve their problems by themselves at school really. They don't try and go for help. They get help from their friends and not from their parents. I find that rather odd."

Sharad at work in the kitchen.

Kiran Ganatra needs no convincing about the value of parental advice and the importance of putting the family first. He states quite simply: "We are prepared to serve our relatives and parents."

Caste

In the "Vedas", Hindu society is described as a corporate state in which people are divided into four classes, or castes, according to male occupation. (The word "caste" has gained common usage in English, but the original Sanskrit word is *varna*.) The four classes are: the *brahmins*, who are scholars and priests (the head of the corporate state); the *kshatryas*, who are the rulers and defenders of the state (the arms); the *vaishyas* who are the businessmen, traders and providers (the belly); and the *shudras*, who are the labourers and agricultural workers (the legs).

If your father was a trader, but you became a scholar, then he was a *vaishya* and you were a *brahmin*. In other words, caste was earned. There was nothing hereditary about the system, nor was it intended to be hierarchical in any way. In fact, the four classes were considered to be in an interdependent relationship with each other.

However, in the middle of the Vedic period, the *brahmis*, who saw a way of turning the situation to their own advantage, introduced the notion that the structure was really a heirarchical one, with themselves at the top and the *shudras* at the bottom. This meant that people now went out of their way to avoid loss of status. If your father was a *kshatrya* but you were a trader, your family were likely to insist that, by upbringing, you were a *kshatrya* too. People also married "within caste" and observed practices prescribed by the *brahmins* in order to maintain their social status. So caste became a question of "breeding".

From here it was a short step to making a connection between social organisation and religion. People were encouraged to assume that being born into a particular caste was an indication of spiritual progress over previous lives. The higher the caste, the more spiritually advanced the individual. Consequently, "caste credentials" became a matter of pride. This is why Ratilal Ganatra, for instance, points out that his family are direct descendants of Lord Rama, and Sharad Rohatgi says that her family were "by caste, born to worship Lord Shiva."

The caste system, in a much elaborated form with many subdivisions within the four main castes, has continued up until the present day. In India, because of the efforts of the government since Independence, its hold is gradually weakening. In Britain, because of the influence of the western style of life, the trend is even more rapid.

Many Hindus are uncertain what to make of this. They accept that the breakdown of the system is inevitable and that "caste doesn't matter any more." At the same time, like Parshotam Kapila, they believe that: "Caste is in the blood. Being of good caste means having good habits, good thoughts, a right way of living." Overall, among the older generation, there is a general air of resignation – a feeling that just because something is breaking down doesn't mean it wasn't valid in the first place.

Marriage

Traditionally, Hindu marriages are arranged. There is no religious justification for this. The practice seems to have arisen through a combination of circumstances.

To avoid the consequences of inbreeding, Hindus do not marry within the family. In rural India, because of the close-knit nature of the village community, this means that they do not normally marry within the village either. In the past, these factors, coupled with the preference for marrying within caste, meant that suitable marriage partners were likely to live at some distance from each other. The young people themselves had no way of meeting, so in the circumstances, arranging marriages must have seemed like the obvious solution.

Very often, match-making was carried out by the village menfolk when they took goods to market. Here, enquiries could be made as to whose son was available to marry whose daughter. Once a prospective match had been identified, the two families concerned would make a thorough investigation into each other's background and general standing. This would include visiting each other's homes. If everything seemed to be in order, then the match would be made. Sometimes the bride and groom would be permitted to see each other before the marriage and sometimes not. On marriage, the bride took her husband's family name and, after a preparatory period, moved in with her husband's family.

The bride and groom at a Hindu wedding.

From a modern European point of view, the concept of arranged marriages can seem somewhat shocking. It seems counter to the idea of romantic love and the freedom of the individual to chose a partner. However, the argument in favour of arranged marriages is a common-sense one. It goes like this: marriages are most likely to succeed where the partners are evenly matched in terms of background, education, temperament and interests. Young people do not have the experience of life and the maturity to be the best judges of who will make a suitable lifelong partner. Parents are the people best placed to do this. Apart from being mature adults with the benefit of experience behind them, they also know their children intimately and can tell what is likely to suit them.

This kind of match-making also used to be the norm in Europe among upper-class families with family reputation and fortunes to be maintained.

Today, in the west, many ordinary people subscribe to computer dating systems. They are really paying for a computer to do the work that in Hindu society would normally be carried out by parents.

Throughout the Hindu community world-wide, the system of match-making is more flexible than it used to be. Even in India, "love matches" are sometimes tolerated. Arranged marriages both there and here usually involve the girl and boy having a chance to meet and talk to each other at least once before the ceremony. Each party has the option of turning the other down if they don't think the match will work. These days, because the Hindu community is so far-flung, the search for suitable partners is often conducted via advertisements in the press, at home and abroad. Matches made in this way are more accurately described as "parentally guided" rather than arranged.

Finding a marriage partner is another potential source of conflict for young British Hindus and their

Wembley: women selling jewellery in the street.

parents.) In some cases, young people have been influenced by the ideas of romantic love and freedom of choice which are promoted heavily through popular media such as films and magazines. Their parents, on the other hand, have remained sceptical, preferring the traditions they are familiar with. This has led to conflict and sometimes violence. Many Hindus are reluctant to talk about this publicly. They feel it involves a loss of face in the eyes of the white community whereas, because of the strength of their family traditions, they ought to be setting a good example.

Both Anita and Rajesh Kapila have friends who are entering arranged marriages about which they have no choice. Many families, though, opt for the parentally guided match as the strategy most likely to succeed.

In all four families featured here, the parents have given up altogether any idea of arranging marriages, and are relying on their children to find their own partners. The Ganatras expect their children to wait until they have finished their studies before getting married. By then, they will be old enough to make a sensible choice which will only need parental approval. This is the way things have already happened with Chandrakant.

In her own case, Indumati Pandya explains: "I wouldn't [arrange a marriage] for my daughter because she's brought up here; I don't think she would accept it." Santosh Kapila states emphatically: "I don't believe in arranged marriages. They're always on the boy's terms. The girl goes to the highest bidder and it's not your parents who have to live with the guy – *you* do."

How do the children feel about this? Alpa agrees with her mother: "It wouldn't work for me. I'm too emancipated in the way I think. I'm too much for letting people do their own thing. I wouldn't allow someone to manipulate me that way. I feel a lot of these Indian girls are manipulated when they have arranged marriages.

"For somebody that had been brought up in a society where boys and girls are separate, arranging marriages might seem quite normal, but where I've been brought up there's a lot of interaction with boys – just as much as with girls.

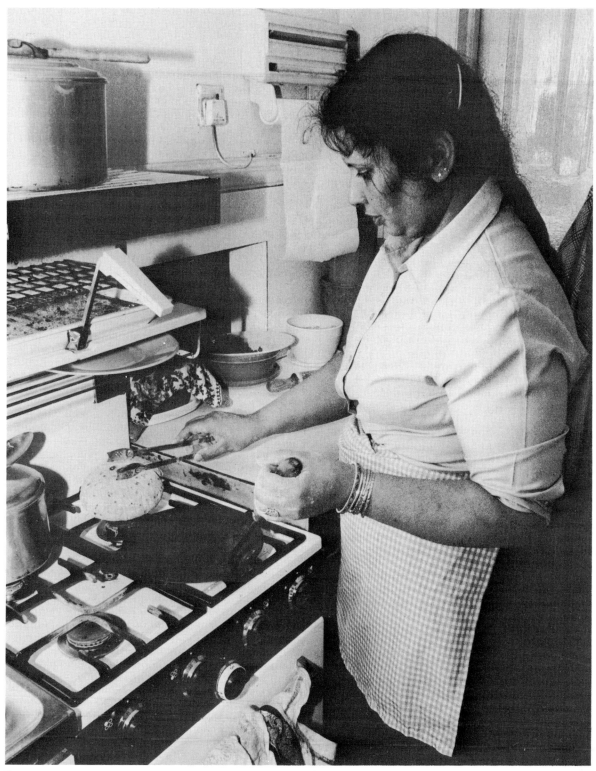

Santosh making *chapattis*.

"I'm determined not to make it [marriage] as cold and impersonal as I've seen it around me. I don't want it to seem as if it's two families marrying each other. That doesn't appeal to me at all."

Anita is quite happy to let things drift. She reckons she would ruin a man's life at the moment because she's more interested in a career than in marriage, "which seems," she says "to involve a lot of blazing rows about mortgages!" She believes that in the fullness of time "you just happen into marriage. You find someone whom you like and who likes you."

Sharad Rohatgi goes as far as to say of her sons: "They're free to marry anybody. I'm not going to interfere. I've nothing against any religion or colour."

Most other parents, though, while making no stipulations that their children should marry within caste, are anxious that they should at least marry Hindus. The reason for this is that parents are afraid that marrying outside the Hindu community will weaken family bonds. Ratilal Rohatgi puts it this way: "The consequence of mixed marriage will be estrangement from both cultures. And our tradition is such that you can't survive without it for the whole of your life."

Generally speaking, the expectation is that there will be no sex before marriage.

The Position of Women

Many people in Britain are under the impression that white women are much more "liberated" than women of Asian origin. This is an assumption which needs careful examination. The fact is that Britain, India, Uganda etc. are all patriarchal societies. This means that men dominate public life, and for the most part control the wealth and own the property.

Manu, who produced India's first Law Code in the period 200 B.C.–A.D.300 setting out the rules of life in Hindu society, wrote: "In childhood a female must be subject to her father, in youth to her husband, when her lord is dead to her sons; a woman must never be independent." (*Chapter V, verse 148*)

In most Hindu households when a decision has to be taken, discussions may range far and wide, but in the end it is the husband who has the authority to decide. This is no different from the situation in most white British families.

Traditionally, Hindu women married early and had their children early in their marriage. From then on, their time was spent running the home. In doing this, they usually had the support of the other women in the joint or extended family, and in many cases, there were also servants to help with the domestic chores. All of the women who feature in this book came from homes where there were servants to do much of the work.

The lives of many Hindu women still follow this pattern. Madhukanta Ganatra believes that the role these women fulfil is a very important one. They create a safe anchorage to which children can always return "without having to make an appointment."

In this situation, where a woman's only sphere of operation is the home, Hindu men sometimes recognise the importance of their role and respect it in a way that many white British men do not. Some Hindu women do go out to work, of course. In Britain the percentage is not as high as among white women. The figure is likely to rise with the next generation, though. Alpa, Anita and Bhavna are all being educated for "independence" and "self-sufficiency". The possibility of having a career is perhaps seen – by parents, rather than by children – as a safety-net should times get hard.

Those women who are already in jobs usually find themselves working double-shifts – one at the shop, or office, or wherever, and another at home. "It's a very, very hard life here," says Indumati Pandya. "I have no leisure time and no interests."

Nevertheless, Santosh, Sharad and Indumati all get a definite satisfaction from being wage-earners. "I get pleasure from being independent," says Santosh, "and not living off money borrowed from relatives." "I enjoy being my own boss," says Indumati.

This is a sensation they share with white women in the same situation. However, there is a long way to go before British women – Hindu or otherwise – have the same status, rights, power and earning potential as men.

7

Hinduism as a Way of Life – Practice and Pastime

Keeping Clean

Personal hygiene is an important aspect of the Hindu way of life, especially as the body is regarded as the physical manifestation of the *Atman*. This means that every day has to start with the bowels being emptied. You can't set about doing anything else until this has been done. Some people have a cup of tea as soon as they wake up to start the process off. Hindus consider that only animals would eat the first meal of the day without ejecting the waste matter from the day before.

In some Hindu homes, a bottle of water is kept next to the lavatory. This serves the same purpose as toilet paper – it is there so that you can clean yourself once the bowels have been emptied. The practice is to reserve the left hand for doing this and to use the right hand for eating food.

In India, using water instead of toilet paper is the usual thing to do. But Britain is a much damper country than India, and moisture doesn't disappear so quickly. This can cause discomfort. Also Hindus in Britain have got used to the idea that people around them use toilet paper. Children, for example, have to adapt to the situation they find at school. As a result, bottles of water appear in fewer and fewer Hindu homes.

Once the bowels have been emptied, the next thing is to clean the teeth. After this, the tongue is cleaned. This is done by using a tongue-scraper. Tongue-scrapers are narrow strips of plastic or metal. The plastic ones can be bent by the user: the metal ones are a ready-made curved shape. When the sharp edge of the tongue-scraper is drawn across the tongue, it removes the fur which has accumulated overnight. the edge of a tea-spoon will do the same job, though not as efficiently.

India – Hindu and Sikh bathing at a tube well. Bathing is a necessary part of daily routine whatever the circumstances.

Some people also clean out their nasal passages at this point. They do this by sniffing water and exhaling it.

Next comes bathing. The general preference is for washing in running water. Hindus who came to Britain in the 1950s and 1960s were horrified to discover the British habit of soaking yourself in a bathful of water containing your own dirt. Most people arrange things so that they can have either a shower or a bucket bath. For the latter, you fill a bucket with clean water and use a jug to pour the water over yourself. This explains why in many Hindu homes, there are plastic buckets and jugs standing about in the bathroom.

Those people who do *puja, hatha yoga* or meditation generally do it after bathing, in preparation for the rest of the day.

Hindus are taught that suppressing the natural bodily functions is harmful. Therefore, in some circles, belching or clearing the nasal passages without apology is in order. The white British, on the other hand, have been taught that it is polite to suppress the noises associated with bodily functions. This is a classic example of an area where cross-cultural misunderstanding can arise. The white British think the Hindus are impolite, and feel repelled. The Hindus think the white British are full of poisons – and feel exactly the same. An effort of will and reason has to be made on both sides to overcome misgivings on this count.

Other "western" habits which would not be tolerated in a fastidious Hindu home are: sharing a drinking vessel with someone else (Holy Communion or Mass as practised by the Christian Church would be detestable to a Hindu, for instance); sampling food from a cooking pot and then putting the utensil back into the pot; washing up in a sink full of static water instead of running water (Sharad Rohatgi recalls her disgust the first time she saw this), and blowing mucus from your nose into a handkerchief and then carrying it around in your pocket all day.

Although the traditional practices described here are widely observed among Hindus in Britain, they are better known among the older generation than among the younger one. Young Hindus, to varying degrees, are adopting the habits of their white contemporaries.

Eating

Indian food is now quite well known in Britain. There is an Indian restaurant in practically every high street and there are many Indian recipe books available in the shops.

A large number of Hindus are vegetarians. Meat is thought to create impurities in the system which make it difficult to pursue spiritual development. Vegetarianism which, in this case, excludes the eating of fish and eggs, is also a logical extension of *ahimsa* (non-violence); see Chapter 5.

In India, it is vegetarianism rather than meat-eating which is the norm. On an Indian train, for instance, you will automatically be offered a choice of menus – one for vegetarians and one for meat-eaters. One reason for the respect which Hindus have for the cow is that it is an important provider of vegetarian food. In Britain it is women, in particular, who are staunch vegetarians.

India – chicken being cooked in a *tandoor* (clay oven). ▷

British food twice a week, and Alpa confesses to a taste for French and Italian food as well. Ravi Rohatgi is even more radical. He says: "My mum cooks [Indian food] but I don't like it. I prefer junk food. I've lived here so long, I think I've just got used to what I've eaten here. They usually cook me separate meals at home."

Keeping Well

There are several systems of medicine practised in India. One of these is the "Ayurvedic" system which, as its name indicates, dates back to the Vedic period.

According to Ayurvedic theory, the body is made up of several "humours" – air, fire and water – which must be maintained in a balanced relationship to each other. Illness occurs when the balance is upset. There are several kinds of remedy aimed at restoring balance to the body. These include incantation, herbal medicines and adjustments of diet. Diet is important because certain foodstuffs stimulate the production of one or other of the humours in the body. Meat, eggs and nuts, for example, are known as "hot" foods because they produce heat. Green vegetables and marrows, on the other hand, are known as "cold" foods because they produce cold. (This has nothing to do with the use or non-use of chillies.)

Homoeopathy, which originated in Germany in the nineteenth century, is also popular in India. In this system, like is treated with like. The medicines produce in a healthy person the very symptoms they cure in a sick person. The more miniscule the dose, the more powerful the effect. Administering the right medicine stimulates the body's own immune system into action, and the patient recovers. (Vaccination works on the same principle.)

Allopathic (western-style) medicine is also practised, but is more expensive for the patient than either of the other two systems.

In Britain, some Hindus still opt for Ayurvedic or homoeopathic treatment when they are ill. In every large Asian community there are likely to be Asian doctors who can offer treatment of these kinds. However, many Hindus have lost touch with or are unaware of this aspect of their heritage. Most would go to an allopathic doctor if they were ill. In fact, a

The typical Hindu diet comprises dishes made from pulses and beans – lentils, chick peas, kidney beans, etc. – and vegetable dishes in which the vegetables are most often fried. Additionally, meat-eaters eat dishes made with mutton, chicken or eggs. Beef and pork are not cooked. (In parts of India, fish is commonly eaten, but this is not the case in Britain.) To all these dishes herbs and spices such as garlic, coriander, turmeric, chillies, ginger, cinnamon, cumin and funnel are added to give flavour and aid digestion. Salad and yoghurt are often served as accompaniments. These dishes are eaten with rice or with forms of bread such as *chapattis, puris, parathas* or *nan.*

Food is usually eaten off *thalis* – stainless steel platters – with *kaulis* – small stainless steel pots – for each dish. People eat with a spoon or with their fingers. The advantage of using your fingers is that you can tell what temperature the food is before putting it in your mouth.

On the whole, the older generation of Hindus in Britain tend to be conservative about their diet and show little curiosity about what other people eat. Nevertheless, women who go out to work do begin to exchange recipes with their white colleagues and to learn about convenience foods. Children find out at school about the standard British repertoire of meals.

In the Rohatgi, Pandya and Kapila families, both Indian and British food is eaten. The Pandyas eat significant number of Hindus living in Britain are actually trained in various aspects of allopathic medicine themselves. This is true in the Rohatgi, Ganatra and Kapila households. Here knowledge and interest in any alternatives is non-existent.

Some old habits die hard, though. For minor ailments, Indumati Pandya uses remedies which have been handed down from generation to generation. These include giving milk with turmeric and butter added for a cold; yoghurt for diarrhoea, and king cumin seeds with salt for indigestion. "You would have to be seriously ill," she says, "before you went to a western-style doctor."

Fun and Games

Wherever there is a sizeable Hindu community in Britain, there are many communal events. These are either religious or cultural in nature. Examples include celebrations of religious festivals such as Dussehra, displays of Indian classical dance, recitals of classical and other styles of music and recitations of poetry.

Whatever the main purpose of these events, they fulfil an important secondary function; they provide people with an opportunity to socialise and to maintain contact with each other. Other than this, where people have their relatives nearby or within travelling distance, the family is an important focus for social activity. In a large family, there are always births, betrothals and marriages to bring people together. But apart from special events, family members simply meet to chat and exchange views.

Ratilal Ganatra and friends engage in earnest discussion △ at a religious event.

Indian classical dance being taught at the Roundabout International Centre, Edinburgh. ▽

India – the newest film releases are heavily advertised.

Bombay has a film industry bigger than the one in Hollywood. The films it produces are as popular among Indians in Britain as among those in India itself. Going in a family group to the cinema to see these films used to be a favourite pastime. Now many families have their own video machines so they can watch them at home.

Food is considered an essential element of any Hindu gathering. Popular snack foods include: *samosas* – pastry envelopes stuffed with vegetables or meat; *pakoras* – deep fried vegetables in batter; *tikki* – potato patties, and *pani puris* – deep fried pastry shells filled with tamarind sauce. Rich sweetmeats such as *burfi* and *gulab jamun* are also popular.

However, things are not the same for everyone. Some of the older generation, like Krishna and Sharad Rohatgi and Kiritkumar and Indumati Pandya, either work too long hours or are too isolated from other Hindus to be part of this social circle. In some cases, as with the Kapilas, even when there is the possibility of taking part, there is no desire to do so. Since coming to Britain, their interest in such activity has waned.

For the younger generation, things are different from the way they were for their parents. Having had some or all of their upbringing in Britain, they have the same interests as their white counterparts.

Sport is very popular in all of our four families, and American football, in particular, is an all-consuming preoccupation. In the Rohatgi family Rahul and Roshan share an interest in American football and golf, both of which they play a lot. Roshan also plays rugby regularly. Ravi Rohatgi has inherited an interest in cricket from his mother whose ambition as a teenager was to be the first woman cricket umpire. (Someone else beat her to it!)

Amit Pandya is another keen American footballer. As well as this, he also plays rugby and is goalie for his school. Both of the younger children – Roshan and Amit – enjoy reading and playing computer games. Amit also keeps exotic fish which he looks after himself. "They're lovely, lovely things," he

Rahul using the Rohatgi boys' home computer.

Ravi Rohatgi plays snooker in the boys' games room.

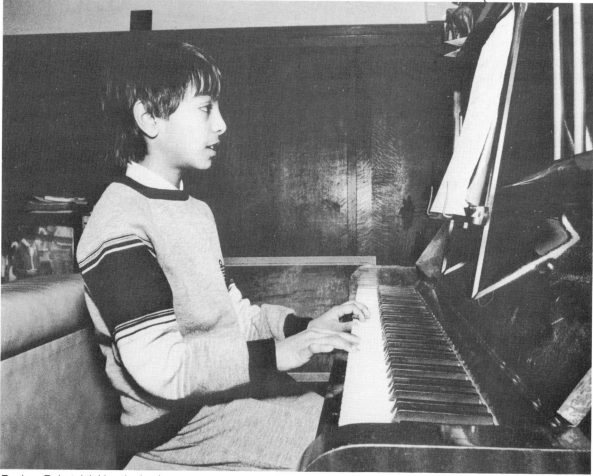

Roshan Rohatgi tinkles the ivories.

says, "gliding about." From Amit's bedroom he can see the gas flame of the Mossmoran oil refinery in Fife. One of his main pastimes, he says, is looking at this flame which is "like a firework" and dreaming.

Rajesh Kapila is an avid snooker player, and spends a lot of his spare time at a private snooker club. He also enjoys listening to rock music, by performers like the Police and Sting.

Alpa Pandya and Anita Kapila are both interested in the theatre. Alpa goes to a lot of events at the Edinburgh Festival, while Anita goes to the theatre in London's West End whenever she can. Alpa also plays basketball. Her other main interest is modern languages. Anita is musically inclined. She plays the recorder, listens to a lot of western classical music and would like to further her musical studies.

As children grow older, the more time they seem to spend at their friends' houses, chatting and watching television. Sometimes – like the older Rohatgis, who are now young adults – their social life includes going to discos or out for a drink. It is inevitable that because they share these interests with other young people who are white, the up-and-coming generation of Hindus feel, in some ways, much closer to the white community than their parents do.

8

Being Brown in Britain

A Sense of Identity

Whenever people migrate to a new country, it takes a while for them to adapt. Things have been no different for the Hindus who came to Britain. First-generation settlers always have memories of another place. Whatever they do, they wonder, "Is this the way we would have done it back in the old place?"

Parshotam Kapila waxes emotional when he says, "There is nothing there [i.e. in India] for us. What I am, I am due to this country. It is my country." However, for the majority of older Hindus, the first loyalty is to Hindu culture – the Hindu way of life. This explains why many regard themselves first and foremost as Indian rather than British, or as Hindus living in Britain rather than British Hindus. This can be true even for people like Indumati Pandya who was born and brought up in an African country and has never been to India.

For people who have this view of themselves, there is no conflict between being a Hindu and being a British citizen. Hinduism acknowledges the importance of good citizenship wherever you are. Nevertheless, it means that there is a sense in which the older generation of Hindus are "half-in and half-out" of British society – a part of it and yet apart from it.

For the younger generation, the situation is different but no less complicated. As we have seen, because of their education and interests, they have much more in common with their white counterparts than their parents do. But being exposed to one culture at home and another at school, or being brown yourself while those around you are white can cause you to ask some pretty serious questions about who you are. Many young Hindus have difficulty in labelling themselves as either British or Indian. Ravi Rohatgi gives some examples of how the problem presents itself to him:

"Sometimes I go out for a meal to an Indian restaurant with my mum and dad. And they order the food, and they can speak Indian, and I feel as if I'm out of place because I can't speak a word of it. (Ravi's mum and dad are probably using Hindi, though their mother tongues are Marathi and Hindi respectively.) Then they have the food and it's spicy and I think, 'Oh no, this is horrible!' So they get me something Scottish, like haggis, and I don't like that either.

"Then again, if I'm with a group of [white] friends in town and we see some coloured people walking down the street, and suppose they're Indian and they're talking Indian, me and my friends really laugh it up. There, I feel as if I'm Scottish because I'm different from them in some way, which I'm really not, because I'm the same colour. I can laugh and not feel any anguish. It's only later it sinks in.

"If there was a fight at school and there was Indians involved and there was Scottish people involved, I don't know where I would stand. . . . Though if it came to a Test Match between the English and the Indians, I would probably support the Indian side."

What is the effect of constantly feeling yourself pulled in different directions? Ravi says: "I feel as if I'm in a void, as if I'm the only one of a kind. I'm not really Scottish, but I don't feel as if I'm really Indian either."

Anita Kapila has dealt with the dilemma by trying

to suppress those aspects of herself that are Indian. She has never tried on a sari, and is deeply embarrassed by the fact that at weekends her local high street is transformed into an Indian-style bazaar and thronged with Indians who have come to do their weekly shopping. She refers to Indians or Hindus as "they" rather than "we" though, at the same time, she says, "I have never known an English person really closely."

Alpa Pandya feels that language plays an important part in the question of identity. Asians generally are often conversant in a number of languages. Most of these have been picked up in public life, through doing business with or working alongside people from other communities. But everyone also has a language they prefer to use at home for private matters. This is called a mother tongue. Alpa feels that it is important for parents and children to have the same mother tongue. Her own mother tongue is Gujerati which she learned simultaneously with English. She says:

"The time when we're closest (in our family) is when we're actually speaking Gujerati. I think being able to communicate and say how you feel in your own language brings you a lot closer together. I very seldom feel totally alienated from my folks. There's nothing that makes me feel 'Oh, cringe! die!' – Not at all."

In her case, the strength of this linguistic bond reinforces her perception of herself as Indian.

Alpa seems to have a point. In the Ganatra family, where there appear to be few problems of identity, the linguistic bonds are strong. The Ganatras have a number of languages at their disposal – some brought from India, some acquired in Africa and some in Britain. Everyone can speak at least three. (Ratilal offers six – Gujerati, English, Hindi, Punjabi, Swahili and rusty French). The two languages that everyone has in common are Gujerati and English. But while English tends to be the language of public life, Gujerati is their mother tongue, for use in less formal circles.

In the Rohatgi and Kapila families where the problems of identity are greater, the ties of language are weaker. The Rohatgi children have not picked up their parents' mother tongues at all, while Rajesh and Anita Kapila know enough Punjabi – which is *their* parents' mother tongue – to be able to understand it, but not to speak it.

Racism

Racism, whether subtle or not-so-subtle, is common in Britain. This makes it difficult for anyone with a brown or black skin to forget their "outsider" status, no matter how hard they try.

Rajesh Kapila complains that his secondary school is "a hell on earth" because of racial tensions between Asians and West Indians, but overall, it is the white majority who are in a position to do most damage where ethnic minority groups are concerned.

The National Front was active in Alpa Pandya's secondary school for most of the time she was there. She says: "In about my third and fourth years it was awful. Two-thirds of the school had become skinheads, and it was at this stage that there was rioting in the south of England and Toxteth and everywhere. [At this point] the verbal abuse got pretty bad. At one stage there were National Front stickers on windows and doors and things."

Amit Pandya gets tough treatment now and then from a couple of classmates who push him around and call him "Paki". Because of his Hindu upbringing (*ahimsa* again), his natural tendency is not to fight back. Kiritkumar Pandya has been attacked while working in his shop:

"Last year an Irish guy came into the shop – 'Can I have a Cornetto?' Now the price was on the side of the Wall's ice-cream cabinet – thirty-five pence. The guy just took the Cornetto and started eating – 'How much?' I said, 'Thirty-five pence.' He said, 'No!' I said, 'Just have a look there.' You know what he did? He kicked the price list. He came to me and he just threw the Cornetto on me. He said, 'This is your Cornetto', and BAM! he broke the window.

"Insurance companies are very strict now – they don't cover windows. That window cost me £165 and £22.50 plus VAT for the emergency board. So before I had even made a penny, I had already lost two hundred pounds! You take it as part of your business, but it doesn't solve your problem."

Kiritkumar is convinced that this attack was racially motivated and is very probably right. Proving it is a different matter though. This is one of the difficulties that ethnic minority peoples are up against.

Racial discrimination can also take much less obvious forms than this. A number of people in our four families complain about being stereotyped racially. Sharad Rohatgi says she gets fed up with

EVENING TIMES

READ BY 600,000 SCOTS EVERY DAY

A special news inquiry that will shock . . .

RACISM: OUR HIDDEN PROBLEM

By JIM MORRISON
and BARBARA McMAHON

A SHOCK increase in Glasgow's racial violence is revealed today.

A special Evening Times investigation has uncovered details of a catalogue of horrific attacks on black families.

And it shatters the myth that Glasgow has a race relations record to be proud of.

HATRED

Two independent surveys among Indian, Pakistani and Chinese families in the South of the city showed a massive 96 per cent have suffered some form of racial harassment.

And a further study, commissioned by the Scottish Education Department, paints a grim picture of racism in the classroom.

The Evening Times special six-page "Race Report" today reveals:

- Arson attacks have been carried out on the homes of Asian families.
- Extra strong plastic glass has been fitted in the homes of ethnic families whose

windows have been repeatedly smashed.
- Asian schoolchildren face a daily barrage of abuse and physical attacks at Glasgow's multi-racial schools.

SIX-PAGE REPORT

ONE MAN'S COURAGE
Page 11

NO PLACE TO HIDE
Pages 12 and 13

THE DISCIPLE OF HATE
Pages 14 and 15

GROWING PROBLEM
Page 16

- Chinese and Vietnamese families have been driven from their homes.
- Shops and premises owned by black businessmen are targets for vandals and racist graffiti.

And while these terror attacks are taking place, extremist organisations such as the British National Party are capitalising by encouraging racial hatred among schoolchildren.

Ethnic minority leaders and race relations experts fear Glasgow is heading for a crisis. And they warn that relations between blacks and whites will continue to deteriorate unless urgent action is taken.

They fear a backlash from young Scottish-born Asians who are no longer willing to put up with daily abuse.

WORSE

Education and police bosses, who have also expressed concern, are monitoring the situation.

Strathclyde's Community Relations Council has a growing dossier of complaints of racial harassment.

And Maggie Chetty, senior community relations councillor, said today: "Things have got a lot worse in the last two or three years."

VOICE OF THE TIMES: PAGE 2

going into grocery shops where just because she's brown and wears a sari, other customers assume she's the shopkeeper and ask her the price of tomatoes. Ravi Rohatgi describes a similar kind of experience:

"When my friends at school discuss pop music they say, 'Do you like that record? Do you like this one?' They all ask each other. But when it comes to me, they all start laughing and start saying things like 'Oh, Ravi Shankar!' It's a joke, but it's as if because all Indians are typecast as liking the sitar, I'm supposed to like it as well."

Ravi has come to the conclusion: "[The white British] have this superior feeling. The Bible tells you not to judge people by their appearance. Yet they're quick to judge everyone on what they look like. What they don't actually know is what they really *are* like." Racism leaves its marks. The Kapilas feel that the Hindus living around them are much more traditional in their outlook than Hindus in India. There is probably some truth in this. When people are treated as outsiders, they are obliged to see themselves in this way. They begin to cherish and defend those things that make them different. Ravi Rohatgi again:

"Indians who come over here are broad-minded, but when they see how narrow-minded people over here are, they recoil. It makes me feel as if there's no point in trying to bridge the gap. You might as well just forget it and be whatever they want you to be. It's futile – frustrating. You just feel so sick when [a racial incident] happens."

Kiritkumar Pandya puts it this way: "When you live with respect, integrity and high morals and somebody tries to abuse you, it's like a Rolls Royce worth £200,000 and that car gets a wee dent. After all, it's a dent. It hurts."

Making Changes

There is some protection against racial discrimination under the law. The 1976 Race Relations Act made it illegal to discriminate against people on grounds of race or colour in employment, education, housing and the provision of services. And it is worth knowing, for example, that if you are discriminated against in the workplace, in training, or in applying for jobs, you can take your case to an Industrial Tribunal. (Leaflets are available from your local Job Centre and Unemployment Benefit Office.)

But it is the day-to-day experience of being insulted, underestimated, ignored and excluded – whether this is done intentionally or unintentionally – that most people from ethnic minority groups find wearing.

A multi-racial society will only flourish where it is recognised that on the basis of their common humanity, all members have an equal right to participate in it. In Britain, everyone – black, brown or white – has responsibilities when it comes to changing things so that this is not only generally understood and accepted, but acted upon both publicly and privately. Collectively, people can influence the institutions and structures in our society so that the barriers which prevent the participation of ethnic minority peoples are removed. Employers, for instance, can introduce equal opportunities and positive discrimination policies in the recruitment of staff. (Some employers – local authorities in particular – have already started to do this.) Trade unions and political parties can examine how best to serve the interests of their ethnic minority members. Individually, people can make the effort to be more open-minded in their dealings with each other.

Being in the majority, the white British obviously have a large part to play in all of this, but ethnic minorities have their responsibilities too. Kiritkumar Pandya takes a hard line on Asians who, because of their bad experiences, have become inward-looking:

"In some of these places where there are problems with stone-throwing [the Asian families] are sitting in one sitting-room, watching telly and yap, yap, yapping. But if you get talking to the person next door to you, if you mix with them, you get to know each other. There's no problem."

An increasing number of ethnic minority adults are helping to change things by becoming involved in politics at a local government level. In the London Borough of Brent (which is where the Kapila family live), 19 of the 43 Labour councillors are black or brown. This is a higher proportion than anywhere else in the country, though it is still not

◁ The Glasgow *Evening Times* takes a responsible line on racism. (The Glasgow *Evening Times*, 10 June, 1986)

Diwali decorations in Leicester. The bi-lingual greeting helps foster good race relations.

representative of the situation in Brent as a whole, where Whites are actually the minority group. Five of the 60 councillors on Leicester's Labour-controlled council are Asian. The council tries hard to run the city on multi-cultural lines. Every year, for instance, the Asian business community and the council between them buy street decorations for Diwali celebrations.

There has been less success at central government level where the representation of ethnic minority groups is almost nil. An episode recounted by Ratilal Ganatra helps explain why.

In the 1984 General Election, Ratilal wanted to stand as Labour member for Leicester East where there is a large Asian community. However, the Labour Party would not agree. They offered him a constituency elsewhere where there was no ethnic minority community and where, realistically, he had no chance of winning. In the event, Ratilal stood as the Independent candidate for Leicester East. The result was that he attracted half the Labour vote, allowing the Conservative to get in which was not what either he or the Labour Party wanted. In Ratilal's opinion, the Labour Party's attitude on this occasion demonstrates the kind of institutional racism which prevents progress being made. This is clearly the kind of case where the white community needs to re-think its strategies. (In fact in the 1987 General Election, the Labour Party selected an Asian, Keith Vaz, to contest the Leicester East seat for them. He won it, to become one of four ethnic minority MPs in the new parliament. On the other hand, at its 1987 conference, the Labour Party voted

Ratilal Ganatra's election poster. ▷

VOTE & CANVASS

FOR YOUR INDEPENDENT ETHNIC MINORITY PARLIAMENTARY CANDIDATE

RATILAL V. GANATRA

આપનો અમૂલ્ય મત
આપના લઘુમતિ સમાજના પાર્લામેન્ટના
સ્વતંત્ર ઉમેદવાર રતિલાલ ગણાત્રાનેજ
આપશો

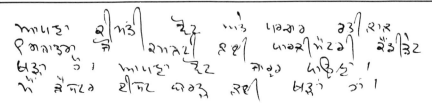

Published by: Nigel David Jealous, 47 Belgrave Road, Leicester   Printed by: The Duplicating Centre, 5 Buller Road, Leicester.

against the creation of a black section to represent ethnic minority interests.)

Education is something which affects everyone. For this reason alone, it could be a powerful tool in the process of change. All ethnic groups, whether small or large, need the opportunity to learn more about their own and each other's cultures. Only then can they make informed comparisons. Only then will they have a level of understanding on which to base personal relationships. An education of this sort could provide people with the chance to learn more about countries like India, to understand the philosophies that underpin different religions and, perhaps, to learn an ethnic minority language.

As things stand, practice varies widely from school to school. At Bhavna Ganatra's state comprehensive you can do a GCE 'O' level in Gujerati if you want. At Ravi Rohatgi's private school you learn nothing specifically intended to equip you for life in a multi-racial society. Ravi says: "We get taught country dancing, British History, British Geography. . . . They could change the system in a way that both sides would benefit by finding out about each other. But they haven't really done that, so all I know is what they [the British] are like."

Alpa Pandya says of her former school, a state comprehensive: "Tolerance was just not taught. [Race Relations] was one of those taboo subjects. Sex was talked about more fully than racial discrimination."

Asians themselves have mixed views about whether or not the education system should be changed. All the parents in our four families are agreed that the education of their children is of vital importance. Kiritkumar Pandya sums it up when he says: "I don't want them struggling like me, selling bananas and apples."

Because of their experience in countries where the safety-net of social security did not exist, and because of the harsh realities they had to cope with when they came to Britain, for most Asian parents education is a question of making sure that you will be able to earn a living for the rest of your life. Vocation doesn't enter into it. Children are encouraged to opt for professions such as accountancy and medicine which are known to pay well and which will always be in demand.

When it comes down to it then, most Asian parents want for their children exactly the same education which has put white Europeans at the top of the tree economically and politically for so long. Parshotam Kapila argues: "Nehru didn't come here to study Hindi. He studied what would enable him to become a world leader."

At the same time, some people are uneasy about things the way they are – Indumati Pandya for one: "I think people should be taught about each other more. They should get together more and talk about their interests." Alpa Pandya recommends: "[Race Relations] should become part of Social Education, just as Careers is. No matter where you stay in the country, you've just got to talk about it. There should be workshops, discussions, visits from the Community Relations Council. . ."

Ravi Rohatgi puts the case this way: "Only from my parents do I know slightly what Indians can be like. If I'm getting a narrow view, it shows that my friends at school will have a very narrow one. Maybe the only Indian they know is me, and I feel as though I'm Scottish. Apart from that they might go to an Indian restaurant. So that's all they're ever going to think – that all Indians do is make food with spices. That's where education could help."

9

The Future

There is no doubt that Hindus, and Asians generally, have established themselves as a part of the economic fabric of British society. Through diligence, enterprise and mutual support, they have managed to carve out a living for themselves. Some of the older generation still think nostalgically sometimes of life in India or in Africa – the sunny weather, the relaxed pace of life, the throngs of people milling sociably on the street as the sun goes down – but this is a vision that is fading.

The future of the younger generation of Hindus seems assured here too, materially at least. Many are now well established in trades or in professions such as medicine and the law. Those who are still studying have clear career ambitions. All, practically without exception, are committed to life in western industrial society, and all, because of their conscientious studying, are likely to find a role in it.

Despite the barrier of racial prejudice, some mingling of cultures is taking place. Asians are impressed by those aspects of the British way of life which demand a high degree of organisation, such as department stores and British television. Organisations and systems which are meant to serve the common good are valued particularly highly. Examples include: the public transport system (before de-regulation, the selling-off of publicly owned services to private companies); mechanisms for regulating traffic flow, including traffic lights, signposts, and so on; care for the handicapped, and the National Health Service generally. The older generation, having come from countries where these things exist in a more rudimentary form, do not take them for granted. In fact, Parshotam Kapila once had to have an operation in a British hospital and was totally bowled over by the attention he received.

There is also admiration for the personal attributes needed to make such highly organised systems work – punctuality, regularity and discipline, for example. The fact that many well-known high street firms offer jobs where the worker's role and responsibilities are clearly defined is something else which some Asians find attractive compared with the small Asian business, where it is sometimes not clear to the worker where the job ends and exploitation begins.

Through being exposed to the same education system and the same popular culture as their white peers, young Asians are beginning to want the same sort of things from life. As Ratilal Ganatra puts it: "They all want to go on holiday to Greece, not to India."

The white British, on the other hand, have gone overboard on Indian food, keeping Indian restaurants in business and cooking it themselves. There is also a growing interest in Indian arts – various forms of classical dance and music in particular. People are learning not just to appreciate these things, but to do them themselves. Since the 1970s, *hatha yoga* has been popular in Britain, and various forms of it are taught at centres up and down the country. More recently, Indian films have begun to appear with greater regularity on British television. At Bhavna Ganatra's school and at others like it where people are doing their best to take multi-culturalism seriously, the women teachers wear saris on the days of Hindu festivals.

All of this is fine as far as it goes. The process of assimilating various aspects of each other's ways of

White students learning the rudiments of Indian classical music from an Indian teacher at the Roundabout International Centre, Edinburgh.

life is inevitable and will accelerate with each succeeding generation.

However, the experience is a different one depending upon whether you are brown or white. Besides picking up information about the outward aspects of the British way of life – dress, food, etc. – young Hindus also unconsciously absorb the values that underpin life here. They have no choice. Through the press, television, advertisements, films and so on, our environment is filled with messages about how people are expected to relate to each other, and what are the good things in life. Once they have absorbed these values, young Hindus then have to reconcile them with the values that operate at home. Either consciously or unconsciously, with or without parental support, they have to decide what course to steer for themselves.

For the white British, the situation is very different. They can *choose* to cultivate an interest in those aspects of Hindu culture that appeal to them. For most people, this means learning about the tangible aspects of life – how to cook tandoori chicken, where to buy okra, how to wear a sari, the name of director Satyajit Ray's first film, and so on.

Neither community is used to asking itself, "What do we believe in that is worth passing on to other people?", and "Do our beliefs stand the test of time?" If the white community are seriously interested in multi-culturalism, they are under a moral obligation to ask themselves these questions. For Hindus the issue is whether or not they are really satisfied with a situation where the superficial aspects of their culture are the only ones which are understood to some degree.

After all, the most valuable contribution which Hindus have to make to any society is Hinduism itself – Hinduism the religion – its analysis of the nature of human existence; its wealth of practical guidance on how to achieve spiritual enlightenment, and the experience of those who have achieved it.

Unfortunately, the older generation of Hindus have done a poor job of passing on the insights of

Book List

.K.S. Iyengar, *Light on Yoga*, Unwin Paperbacks, 1966

Mary Lutyens (ed.), *The Penguin Krishnamurti Reader*, Penguin, 1970

arvepalli Radhakrishnan and Charles A. Moore (eds.), *A Sourcebook in Indian Philosophy*, Princetown University Press, 1957

Bhagwan Shri Rajneesh, *The Secret of Secrets* (Volume 2), Rajneesh Foundation International, 1983

Bhagavad Gita, adapted by Yogi Ramacharaka, Yogi Publication Society, 1930

D.S. Sharma, *Hinduism Through the Ages*, Bharatiya Vidya Bhavan, 1967

Romila Thapar, *A History of India 1*, Penguin, 1966

Acknowledgments

The drawing on page 8 is by Davy Hunter. The maps on page 12 and 13 were drawn by Naresh Sohal. Parshotam Kapila loaned the photograph which appears on page 16 (*top left*). Kiritkumar Pandya loaned the photographs on page 18. The *Dalkeith Advertiser* and the Glasgow *Evening Times* gave kind permission for the use of the extracts on page 20 and page 54. Ratilal Ganatra donated the poster reproduced on page 57.

Useful Addresses

Commision for Racial Equality
Elliot House,
10-12 Allington Street, London SW1E 5EH

High Commission of India
India House
Aldwych, London WC2

Hindu Centre
39 Grafton Terrace
off Malden Road
Chalk Farm, London NW5 4JA

Indian Workers Association
Dominion Centre
112 The Green
Southall
Middlesex UB2 4DF

Institute of Race Relations
247 Pentonville Road, London N1

Minority Rights Group
29 Craven Street, London WC2N 5NT

Hinduism to their children. In some cases, they have introduced them to the superficialities of religion – the rituals and ceremonies – but not the underlying concepts, perhaps because of a lack of confidence in their own abilities as teachers. In some cases, not wanting to interfere with their children's experience of growing up in Britain, they have taken a *laissez-faire* ("let be") attitude, assuming that their children will learn what is most appropriate for them.

It is not in the spirit of Hinduism to proselytise – to make recommendations to other people about what they should believe in. If pushed, Ratilal Ganatra will say that he thinks the white British could from the Hindu family structure but w further than that. But the time is fast con Hindus in Britain will have to be explicit a they believe in. Either that or they will run being known simply, as Ravi Rohatgi people who make food with spices". Their perspective on life, evolved since be beginnings of recorded history, will be losi to their own descendants, but to British sc whole. And that would be a great loss.

9

The
Future

There is no doubt that Hindus, and Asians generally, have established themselves as a part of the economic fabric of British society. Through diligence, enterprise and mutual support, they have managed to carve out a living for themselves. Some of the older generation still think nostalgically sometimes of life in India or in Africa – the sunny weather, the relaxed pace of life, the throngs of people milling sociably on the street as the sun goes down – but this is a vision that is fading.

The future of the younger generation of Hindus seems assured here too, materially at least. Many are now well established in trades or in professions such as medicine and the law. Those who are still studying have clear career ambitions. All, practically without exception, are committed to life in western industrial society, and all, because of their conscientious studying, are likely to find a role in it.

Despite the barrier of racial prejudice, some mingling of cultures is taking place. Asians are impressed by those aspects of the British way of life which demand a high degree of organisation, such as department stores and British television. Organisations and systems which are meant to serve the common good are valued particularly highly. Examples include: the public transport system (before de-regulation, the selling-off of publicly owned services to private companies); mechanisms for regulating traffic flow, including traffic lights, signposts, and so on; care for the handicapped, and the National Health Service generally. The older generation, having come from countries where these things exist in a more rudimentary form, do not take them for granted. In fact, Parshotam Kapila once had to have an operation in a British hospital and was totally bowled over by the attention he received.

There is also admiration for the personal attributes needed to make such highly organised systems work – punctuality, regularity and discipline, for example. The fact that many well-known high street firms offer jobs where the worker's role and responsibilities are clearly defined is something else which some Asians find attractive compared with the small Asian business, where it is sometimes not clear to the worker where the job ends and exploitation begins.

Through being exposed to the same education system and the same popular culture as their white peers, young Asians are beginning to want the same sort of things from life. As Ratilal Ganatra puts it: "They all want to go on holiday to Greece, not to India."

The white British, on the other hand, have gone overboard on Indian food, keeping Indian restaurants in business and cooking it themselves. There is also a growing interest in Indian arts – various forms of classical dance and music in particular. People are learning not just to appreciate these things, but to do them themselves. Since the 1970s, *hatha yoga* has been popular in Britain, and various forms of it are taught at centres up and down the country. More recently, Indian films have begun to appear with greater regularity on British television. At Bhavna Ganatra's school and at others like it where people are doing their best to take multi-culturalism seriously, the women teachers wear saris on the days of Hindu festivals.

All of this is fine as far as it goes. The process of assimilating various aspects of each other's ways of

White students learning the rudiments of Indian classical music from an Indian teacher at the Roundabout International Centre, Edinburgh.

life is inevitable and will accelerate with each succeeding generation.

However, the experience is a different one depending upon whether you are brown or white. Besides picking up information about the outward aspects of the British way of life – dress, food, etc. – young Hindus also unconsciously absorb the values that underpin life here. They have no choice. Through the press, television, advertisements, films and so on, our environment is filled with messages about how people are expected to relate to each other, and what are the good things in life. Once they have absorbed these values, young Hindus then have to reconcile them with the values that operate at home. Either consciously or unconsciously, with or without parental support, they have to decide what course to steer for themselves.

For the white British, the situation is very different. They can *choose* to cultivate an interest in those aspects of Hindu culture that appeal to them. For most people, this means learning about the tangible aspects of life – how to cook tandoori chicken, where to buy okra, how to wear a sari, the name of director Satyajit Ray's first film, and so on.

Neither community is used to asking itself, "What do we believe in that is worth passing on to other people?", and "Do our beliefs stand the test of time?" If the white community are seriously interested in multi-culturalism, they are under a moral obligation to ask themselves these questions. For Hindus the issue is whether or not they are really satisfied with a situation where the superficial aspects of their culture are the only ones which are understood to some degree.

After all, the most valuable contribution which Hindus have to make to any society is Hinduism itself – Hinduism the religion – its analysis of the nature of human existence; its wealth of practical guidance on how to achieve spiritual enlightenment, and the experience of those who have achieved it.

Unfortunately, the older generation of Hindus have done a poor job of passing on the insights of

Hinduism to their children. In some cases, they have introduced them to the superficialities of religion – the rituals and ceremonies – but not the underlying concepts, perhaps because of a lack of confidence in their own abilities as teachers. In some cases, not wanting to interfere with their children's experience of growing up in Britain, they have taken a *laissez-faire* ("let be") attitude, assuming that their children will learn what is most appropriate for them.

It is not in the spirit of Hinduism to proselytise – to make recommendations to other people about what they should believe in. If pushed, Ratilal Ganatra will say that he thinks the white British could learn a lot from the Hindu family structure but will go no further than that. But the time is fast coming when Hindus in Britain will have to be explicit about what they believe in. Either that or they will run the risk of being known simply, as Ravi Rohatgi says, "as people who make food with spices". Their particular perspective on life, evolved since before the beginnings of recorded history, will be lost not only to their own descendants, but to British society as a whole. And that would be a great loss.

Book List

B.K.S. Iyengar, *Light on Yoga*, Unwin Paperbacks, 1966

Mary Lutyens (ed.), *The Penguin Krishnamurti Reader*, Penguin, 1970

Sarvepalli Radhakrishnan and Charles A. Moore (eds.), *A Sourcebook in Indian Philosophy*, Princetown University Press, 1957

Bhagwan Shri Rajneesh, *The Secret of Secrets* (Volume 2), Rajneesh Foundation International, 1983

Bhagavad Gita, adapted by Yogi Ramacharaka, Yogi Publication Society, 1930

D.S. Sharma, *Hinduism Through the Ages*, Bharatiya Vidya Bhavan, 1967

Romila Thapar, *A History of India 1*, Penguin, 1966

Acknowledgments

The drawing on page 8 is by Davy Hunter. The maps on page 12 and 13 were drawn by Naresh Sohal. Parshotam Kapila loaned the photograph which appears on page 16 (*top left*). Kiritkumar Pandya loaned the photographs on page 18. The *Dalkeith Advertiser* and the Glasgow *Evening Times* gave kind permission for the use of the extracts on page 20 and page 54. Ratilal Ganatra donated the poster reproduced on page 57.

Useful Addresses

Commision for Racial Equality
Elliot House,
10-12 Allington Street, London SW1E 5EH

High Commission of India
India House
Aldwych, London WC2

Hindu Centre
39 Grafton Terrace
off Malden Road
Chalk Farm, London NW5 4JA

Indian Workers Association
Dominion Centre
112 The Green
Southall
Middlesex UB2 4DF

Institute of Race Relations
247 Pentonville Road, London N1

Minority Rights Group
29 Craven Street, London WC2N 5NT

Index